Worship and Evangelism in Pre-Christendom

by Alan Kreider

Research Fellow in Church History
and Director of the Centre for Christianity and Culture,
Regent's Park College, Oxford

THE ALCUIN CLUB and the GROUP FOR RENEWAL OF WORSHIP (GROW)

The Alcuin Club, which exists to promote the study of Christian liturgy in general and of Anglican liturgy in particular, traditionally published a single volume annually for its members. This ceased in 1986 but resumed in 1992. Similarly, GROW was responsible from 1975 to 1986 for the quarterly 'Grove Liturgical Studies'. Since the beginning of 1987 the two have sponsored a Joint Editorial Board to produce 'Joint Liturgical Studies' initially quarterly, now three times a year; details of these are to be found at the end of this Study.

THE COVER PHOTOGRAPH

Shows dove, olive branch, and Orante, Rome (Priscilla epigraph no. 198). This is reprinted by permission from Graydon F. Snyder, *Ante Pacem: Archaeological Evidence of Church Life before Constantine* (Mercer University Press, 1985) p.17.

DEDICATION

For my parents
Carl Kreider
Evelyn Burkholder Kreider

First Impression September 1995
ISSN 0951-2667
ISBN 1 85174 299 9

GROVE BOOKS LIMITED
RIDLEY HALL RD, CAMBRIDGE. CB3 9HU

CONTENTS

ACKNOWLEDGEMENTS

This essay originated as the Laing Lecture for 1994, given in February 1994 at London Bible College, Northwood, Middlesex. I am grateful to LBC's then principal, Dr. Peter Cotterell, for the invitation to give the lecture. It was then published in *Vox Evangelica* 24 (1994) pp.7-38, and is now re-published by permission. Since then I have lengthened the lecture and revised it extensively, but the style remains that of an oral presentation. The insertion of chapter headings in particular, whilst useful for identifying the parts of the presentation, ought not to obscure the flow and continuity of the original.

I would like to thank several people for their help. Rev. Prof. Paul Bradshaw, in several conversations, provided me with valuable bibliographical advice. Other scholars, Rev. S. Anita Stauffer, Prof. Everett Ferguson, Prof. Willard Swartley, and Fr. Eoin de Bhaldraithe, O. Cist., provided detailed criticisms. At every stage my wife, Eleanor Kreider, provided me with advice, criticism and conversation about concerns which we share deeply—worship, evangelism, the Church's social witness, and early Christianity. To all of these I give my sincere thanks. The remaining faults are mine.

1. Introduction

About one thing at least there is no dispute; the pre-Christendom church was growing. Contemporaries commented on it: the late second-century Epistle to Diognetus noted soberly that Christians 'day by day increase more and more.' In the middle of the following century Origen could write without fear of contradiction about 'the multitude of people coming to the faith.'[1] Across the Roman Empire, for those who looked behind the facades, there was evidence of growth. In Rome the first congregations were literally *house* churches. Meeting in the largest rooms of their members who were rarely wealthy, the people attending could rarely have totalled much higher than fifteen or twenty.[2] But by the mid-third century, congregations were growing in numbers and wealth. So Christians, who still met in *insulae* (islands), multi-storied blocks containing shops and housing, unobtrusively began to convert private spaces into domestic complexes tailored to congregational needs. They knocked down walls to unite apartments, thereby creating the varied spaces, large and small, that were required by the lives of their growing communities. The *titulus Byzantis* in Rome as well as the famous *domus ecclesiae* in Dura Europos in Eastern Syria were both, in the words of architectural historian Richard Krautheimer, 'inconspicuous community centres.' In many respects their life was still domestic, but their changing architecture reflected the expanding life and numbers of their communities.[3] It was in such a building in Caesarea that Origen discovered that the growth of the church and its houses could be pastorally problematic: some people, he complained, were playing truant during his daily homilies and had 'hidden in the remotest corners of the house of the Lord [*dominicae domus*], . . . [where they] occupy themselves with profane stories.'[4]

---

[1] *Epistle to Diognetus* 6.9; Origen, *Contra Celsum* 3.9.

[2] Peter Lampe, *Die stadtrömischen Christen in den ersten beiden Jahrhunderten: Untersuchung zur Sozialgeschichte*, Wissenschaftliche Untersuchungen zum Neuen Testament, 2. Reihe, 18 (J. C. B. Mohr [Paul Siebeck], Tübingen, 1987) p.161.

[3] Graydon F. Snyder, *Ante Pacem: Archaeological Evidence of Church Life Before Constantine* (Mercer University Press, Macon, GA, 1985) pp.77-80; L. Michael White, *Building God's House in the Roman World* (Johns Hopkins University Press, Baltimore, 1990) pp.111-114; Richard Krautheimer, *Rome, Profile of a City, 312-1308* (Princeton University Press, 1980) p.33.

[4] Origen, *Homilies on Exodus*, 12.2.

2. Measuring the Church's Growth

Noting the growth is one thing; measuring it is another. To give a very rough impression of 'the dimensions of growth,' ancient historian Ramsay MacMullen of Yale has estimated a growth 'on the order of a half a million in each generation from the end of the first century' up to the conversion of the Emperor Constantine in 312 AD. By that time, MacMullen estimates, the church scattered unevenly across the Empire constituted between five and eight per cent of the imperial population.[1] Other estimates are higher than this. A recent study by Professor Wolfgang Wischmeyer of Erlangen has proposed, astonishingly, that the Christians comprised 'perhaps' twenty to twenty-five per cent of the imperial populace; but this, which might be credible for parts of Asia Minor, is certainly to high for the empire as a whole.[2] It is impossible, at this stage of research, to be sure.

Whatever the figure scholars eventually agree upon, it will bear testimony to growth that was remarkable. For the growth of the church in pre-Christendom took place in the face of imposing disincentives. Lethal persecution was not constant, and many Christians would never experience it directly. But every Christian knew that persecution, because of imperial edict or local crisis, could break out with community-engulfing virulence. So they passed down the acts of the martyrs and celebrated the anniversaries of their deaths which they believed were really *birth* days. They commented on the experiences of being barricaded in their house churches—'beseiged, and attacked, and kept prisoners actually in our secret congregations' is how Tertullian put it—or, as Origen reported, of having their buildings burned down.[3] They knew that 'every Christian by definition was a candidate for death.'[4] To understate: if one wanted a soft life, or to get ahead in respectable circles, one did not become a Christian.

And yet people became Christians. Why? It has intrigued recent historians to test, and rule out, a whole series of reasons which one might expect ought to have been important. Public preaching, for example: there was, as Arthur Darby Nock has emphasized, 'little, if any, direct preaching to the masses;' it was simply too dangerous.[5] Or organizing the congregations for mission: according to Georg Kretschmar, 'the recruitment to the faith was never institutionalized . . . [I]n these communities the social life was in general . . . clearly structured, whereas for the connections "outwards" practically no firm rules are

---

[1] Ramsay MacMullen, *Christianizing the Roman Empire (A.D. 100-400)* (Yale University Press, New Haven, 1984) pp.86, 109-110; cf. Robin Lane Fox, who estimated four to five per cent (*Pagans and Christians* (Harper & Row, San Francisco, 1986) p.592).

[2] Wolfgang Wischmeyer, *Von Golgatha zum Ponte Molle: Studien zur Sozialgeschichte der Kirche im dritten Jahrhundert* (Vandenhoeck & Ruprecht, Göttingen, 1992) p.24. Cf. Stephen Mitchell, *Anatolia: Land, Men, and Gods in Asia Minor*: II, *The Rise of the Church* (Clarendon Press, Oxford, 1993) pp.62-63; Rita Lizzi, 'Ambrose's Contemporaries and the Christianization of Northern Italy' in *Journal of Roman Studies* 80 (1990) p.159.

[3] Tertullian, *Ad Nationes*, 1.7.19; Origen, *Comm on Matthew* 24.9-10, 39.

[4] Gustave Bardy, *La Conversion au christianisme durant les premiers siècles* (Aubier, Paris, 1949) p.170.

[5] Arthur Darby Nock, *Conversion* (Clarendon Press, Oxford, 1933) p.212. Apparent exceptions, such as the Pseudo-Clementine *Recognitions*, 1.6.4f (E. Hennecke and W. Schneemelcher (eds.), *New Testament Apocrypha* (SCM, London, 1973-1974) pp.538-9) are not strong enough to validate Michael Green's assurance that 'there can be no doubt that . . . open-air evangelism continued throughout the first two centuries' (*Evangelism in the Early Church* (Hodder and Stoughton, London, 1970) p.197).

recognizable . . .'[1] How about prayer for the conversion of pagans? Yves Congar has observed that 'the Christians prayed for the prosperity and peace of people, but scarcely for their conversion.'[2] In fact, most of the very few prayers for conversion which survive from the early centuries, eight out of eleven in all according to my count, are prayers in obedience to Jesus' command to pray for enemies and persecutors.[3] As to theologizing of an explicitly missionary nature, 'astonishing' is the only word which for Norbert Brox will adequately describe 'the scarcity of reflection about mission.'[4] To this list of surprising omissions I would like to add one more—the absence of pastoral admonitions to evangelize. A sample of this is *Ad Quirinum* by the North African bishop and martyr Cyprian. The third book of this work is a manual of 120 'heavenly precepts' to guide catechumens in the Christian life. These 'precepts' cover a whole range of areas of Christian concern—'that brethren ought to support one another,' or 'that we are to be urgent in prayers'—but none, not one of the 120, urges the new believers to evangelize.[5]

---

[1] Georg Kretschmar, 'Das christliche Leben und die Mission in der frühen Kirche,' in H. Frohnes and U. W. Knorr (eds.) *Kirchengeschichte als Missionsgeschichte*: I, *Die Alte Kirche* (Chr. Kaiser Verlag, Munich, 1974) p.94.

[2] Y. Congar, 'Souci du salut des païens et conscience missionaire dans le christianisme postapostolique et préconstantinien' in P. Granfield and J. A. Jungmann (eds.) *Kyriakon: Festschrift Johannes Quasten* (Aschendorff, Münster, 1970) I p.5.

[3] 1 Clement 59.4; Ignatius, *Eph* 10.1; Aristeides, *Apol* 17.3; Justin, *Dial* 108.3; *Didascalia Apostolorum* 2.56; Cyprian, *De Oratione dominica* 17; to which Norbert Brox (p.212, see note 4 below), adds Justin, *Dial* 35.8; *Apostolic Constitutions* 8.10.16f. To these I would add Polycarp, *Ep* 12.3; Cyprian, *Ad Demetrianum* 20; Pontius, *Vita Cypriani* 9. Of these, four refer explicitly to Jesus' enemy-loving teaching; five refer implicitly to enemy-loving; and only two (1 Clement 59.4 and Cyprian *Ad Dem* 20) express prayer for conversion of 'all nations' or of an individual on more general grounds.

[4] N. Brox, 'Zur christlichen Mission in der Spätantike' in K. Kertelge (ed.), *Mission im Neuen Testament*, Quaestiones Disputatae, 93 (Herder, Freiburg-im-Breisgau, 1982) p.211. Martin Goodman has argued that, although for many early Christians the commitment to universal proselytizing was only 'implicit' or 'passive', such an understanding had 'quite a profound historical effect' (*Mission and Conversion: Proselytizing in the Religious History of the Roman Empire* (Clarendon Press, Oxford, 1994) pp.159-160).

[5] Cyprian, *Ad Quirinum*, 3, preface, 9, 120. The significance of this work has been missed in part because several late MSS added the subtitle 'Three books of testimonies,' to which 'against the Jews' was sometimes added. See Pierre Monat, 'Les *testimonia* bibliques de Cyprien à Lactance' in Jacques Fontaine and Charles Pietri (eds.), *Le Monde latin antique et la Bible*, Bible de tous les temps, II (Beauchesne, Paris, 1985) p.501.

3. Worship without Evangelism

This is already a formidable list of reasons to rule out for the church's growth, but there is a final one that seems to me to be both important and fascinating: the church did not grow because its worship was attractive.[1] The reason is simple: from the mid-first century onwards pagans were not admitted to Christian worship services. Until non-Christians were willing to submit to the interrogation necessary to become a catechumen, and as a catechumen to be trained for membership in the Christian community, they were not allowed through the door into a Christian worship service. And even then, until they were baptized, they were allowed to stay only for the service of the word—the biblical readings and teaching; they were firmly dismissed before the unitive actions of Christian worship—the prayers and the kiss of peace culminating in the eucharist. Christian worship was thus surrounded by what one historian has called an 'invisible mine field.'[2] Contemporary critics sensed this. Celsus: Christians are 'a secret society'; Caecilius: 'Why do [the Christians] never speak in public, never meet in the open, if it be not that the aspect of their worship is either criminal or shameful?'[3]

At first, of course, pagans had indeed been allowed to attend Christian worship services. Paul, in 1 Corinthians 14, urged his enthusiastic friends to comport themselves in such a way that, when 'outsiders or unbelievers enter', they will 'not say that you are out of your mind' (1 Cor. 14.23). In Corinth it was clearly expected that pagans would come. In this, the early Christians were in the tradition of the Jewish synagogues, which courted outsiders and whose services 'had the functions both of edification and of solicitation.'[4] After the Neronian persecution of the mid-60s, however, the Christian churches seem to have felt it necessary to exclude outsiders. They, unlike the Jews, were now styled a *superstitio*, a deviation from the norms of acceptable behaviour; now they, as Pliny put it in his correspondence with the Emperor Trajan, were subject to execution not only for their 'secret crimes' but also for 'the mere name.'[5] In these circumstances it is hardly surprising that the Christians closed their doors to outsiders; to let just anybody in was simply too dangerous.[6]

The early Christian documents are explicit about this. The believers feared the presence of what Athenagoras of Athens called 'lying informers.'[7] So they, in various

---

[1] The relationship of worship and evangelism in early Christianity has been little discussed. Adolf von Harnack's magisterial *The Mission and Expansion of Christianity in the First Three Centuries*, 2 vols (Williams and Norgate, London, 1904-1908) does not deal with the subject. Gustave Bardy's important work on conversion (*Conversion* pp.280-291) provides some useful observations. But the patristic writers themselves devote little attention to the missionary dimensions of their worship; certainly there was no early Christian equivalent to the recent call by Canon Robert Warren for 'missionary liturgies' (*Church Times*, 15 July 1994 p.10).

[2] MacMullen, *Christianizing* p.104.

[3] Origen, *Contra Celsum* 8.17; Minucius Felix, *Octavius* 10.2.

[4] Dieter Georgi, *The Opponents of Paul in Second Corinthians* (Fortress Press, Philadelphia, 1986) p.90; cf. J. N. Lightstone, *The Commerce of the Sacred: Mediation of the Divine among Jews in the Graeco-Roman Diaspora*, Brown Judaic Studies, 59 (Scholars Press, Chico, CA, 1984) p.12.

[5] Pliny, *Ep* 10.96.2.

[6] 'Christians perform their rites and teach their doctrines in secret . . . they do this with good reason to escape the penalty that hangs over them' (Origen, *Contra Celsum* 1.7).

[7] Athenagoras, *Legatio* 1.3. Origen reported the concern that 'those who indulge in 'trickery' be barred from the Christian gatherings (*Contra Celsum* 3.51).

parts of the Empire, assigned someone to watch at the door to see that only appropriate people came in. Typical of this is the mid-fourth-century *Testament of our Lord*, which describes one of the deacon's functions as that of the ecclesiastical bouncer:

'Let him observe and look at those who come into the house of the sanctuary. Let him investigate who they are, so that he may know if they are lambs or wolves. And when he asks, let him bring in him that is worthy, lest, if a spy enter, the liberty of the Church be searched out, and his sin be on his head.'[1]

Other church orders describe similar duties.[2] In light of this screening process it is unsurprising that, when Origen described those who were present in the congregation in Caesarea to which he was preaching, he spoke of 'all, catechumens and faithful, women, men and children'—but no pagans. They simply weren't there.[3]

So, in pre-Christendom, there was *no connection* between worship and evangelism. It simply didn't matter whether the church's worship was attractive to outsiders. It wasn't designed for outsiders, and outsiders weren't there. The topic that I have set for myself therefore appears to be a *non sequitur*.

---

[1] *Testamentum Domini*, 1.36 (James Cooper and A. J. Maclean (eds.) (T & T Clark, Edinburgh, 1902). This is traditional material, reflecting pre-Christendom practice. The date and place of origin of the document are matters of scholarly debate. I agree with Grant Sperry-White (*The Testamentum Domini: A Text for Students*, Alcuin/GROW Liturgical Study 19 (Grove Books, Bramcote, Notts., 1991) p.6), in locating the document in Asia Minor, in the second half of the fourth century (but before 381), not least because of a reason that Sperry-White does not offer: the prominence of apocalyptic theology and charismatic phenomena that may suggest some kind of continuity with Montanism (1.2-14, 24, 32, 47).

[2] *Didascalia Apostolorum* 2.39 (only pagans who promise to repent, and say 'We believe', are received into the congregation 'that they may hear the word'); *Apostolic Constitutions* 2.39. See also Gregory Thaumaturgus, *Canonical Epistle* 11; Laodicea, Canon 43 (152), and the comments of Origen (*Contra Celsum* 3.51), and Epiphanius (*Panarion* 3.2.21).

[3] Origen, *Homilies on Luke* 32.6.

4. Worship:
Nurturing the 'Enclosed Garden'

And yet I think there was a connection. I believe that worship, to which pagans were denied admission, was all-important in the spread of the church. It was important, not because it was attractive, but because its rites and practices—whether by design or intuition—made a difference in the lives and communities of the worshippers. It performed the function of re-forming those pagans who joined the church into Christians, into distinctive people who lived in a way that was recognizably in the tradition of Jesus Christ. As such these people, re-formed, would be attractive. And not only attractive but free. In an age of bondage, of increasing disorder, of a deepening gulf between privileged people and poor people, and of life-disfiguring addictions and compulsions, the church was growing because it and its members sensed that they had discovered freedom and a way of life, in Christ, that was genuinely alive. This, as I shall seek to demonstrate, was good news, news that was *new*. And this newness in the practices of its corporate life and the behaviour of its members towards non-members was intriguing, inviting, question-posing. Why, people asked, do the Christian live like *that*?

The pre-Christendom Christians often remarked that they had been ushered into a privileged place. The mid-third-century bishop of Carthage, Cyprian, repeatedly referred to it as an 'enclosed garden'.[1] Quoting Song of Solomon 4.12, in which he heard the voice of Christ, he wrote: ' "A garden enclosed [*hortus conclusus*] is my sister, my spouse; a spring sealed up, a well of living water." But if the spouse of Christ, which is the church, is a garden enclosed, a thing that is closed up cannot lie open to strangers and profane persons.'[2] Enclosed: outsiders cannot easily get in. A garden: here is life flowering and flourishing in the presence of Christ. Cyprian and other Christians sought repeatedly to express the delight and the newness of their common life in Christ. 'This is a new people, and there is something divine mingled with it.' This is 'a new race or way of life'. This is 'God's country.' This is 'Paradise'. This is 'the place where the Holy Spirit flourishes.'[3]

---

[1] Cyprian, *Ep* 73(74).11; Firmilian of Neocaesarea, in Cyprian, *Ep* 74(75).15, quoting Cyprian on this theme.

[2] Cyprian, *Ep* 75(69).2.

[3] Aristeides, *Apol* 16; *Epistle to Diognetus* 2; Origen, *Contra Celsum* 8.75; Hippolytus, *Comm on Daniel* 1.17; *Apostolic Tradition* 41, 35.

5. Jesus-Shaped Distinctiveness

The heart of the newness, the pre-Christendom Christians sensed, was the person and teaching of Jesus Christ. He and his words were good news to people. Jesus' words were, according to the mid-third-century *Didascalia Apostolorum*, 'incisive words'.[1] Origen testified that they had a 'charm' that drew people to follow him.[2] In Justin's experience Jesus' words 'possess a terrible power in themselves, and are sufficient to inspire those who turn aside from the path of rectitude with awe; and the sweetest rest is afforded to those who make a diligent practice of them.'[3] Pagans, the Christians testified, were drawn to Jesus and his Sermon on the Mount teachings.[4] The idea that these were hyperbolic demands which were 'unfulfillable' never occurs in their writings.[5] And no teaching was more repeated by the Christians, or more pondered by the pagans, than Jesus' command to love the enemy.[6] Was this because it was part of a 'an extremely early fixed catechetical tradition?'[7] Or was this because, in a situation in which Christians were surrounded by enemies, it gave them a creative way to respond? We do not know.

What we do know is that many pre-Christendom Christians felt themselves to be out of joint with the dominant values of their time. Of course, the Christians were involved in a constant process of 'inculturation'; from classical culture they adopted and adapted vocabulary, visual images, and philosophical categories through which they understood

---

[1] *Didascalia Apostolorum* 6.23.

[2] Origen, *Contra Celsum* 3.10.

[3] Justin, *Dial* 8.

[4] 2 Clement, *Ep* 13.3.

[5] Karlmann Beyschlag, 'Zur Geschichte der Bergpredigt in der Alten Kirche,' *Zeitschrift für Theologie und Kirche* 74 (1977) p.297; R. M. Grant, 'The Sermon on the Mount in Early Christianity,' *Semeia* 12 (1978) pp.215-231.

[6] For example, in Theophilus, *Ad Autolycum*, four of eight explicit New Testament quotations come from Mt. 5-6, and two quote Mt. 5.44 and 5.46; in Athenagoras, *Legatio*, of 23 citations five come from Mt. 5-7, and two of these refer to Mt. 5.44-46. The location of enemy love in the argument of these two works is central: Theophilus, 3.14; Athenagoras, 11.2. In the entire corpus of patristic citations from the Matthew's gospel up through and including Irenaeus, the most quoted verses (both cited 17 times) are Mt 17.5 ('This is my Son,' from the Transfiguration account) and Mt. 5.44 ('Love your enemies'). If one adds the entire pericope of the sixth antithesis (Mt. 5.43-48), the total number of citations rises to 37, making this by far the most frequently cited passage in Matthew. This information comes from the statistical tables in Wolf-Dietrich Köhler, *Die Rezeption des Matthäusevangeliums in der Zeit vor Irenäus*, Wissenschaftliche Untersuchungen zum Neuen Testament, 2. Reihe, 24 (J. C. B. Mohr [Paul Siebeck], Tübingen, 1987) pp.541f. (I owe this reference to Professor Peter Lampe of the University of Kiel.) It would be fascinating to compare this with citations from other New Testament writings. For general reflections on Jesus' love-command in early Christianity, see Walter Bauer, 'Das Gebot der Feindesliebe und die alten Christen,' *Zeitschrift für Theologie und Kirche*, 27 (Ergänzungsheft) (1917) pp.37-54; Eric Osborn, 'The Love Command in Second-Century Christian Writing' in *Second Century*, 1 (1981) pp.223-243.

[7] Walter Wink, *Engaging the Powers* (Fortress Press, Minneapolis, 1993) pp.185-186. See also Victor Paul Furnish, *The Love Command in the New Testament* (SCM Press, London, 1973) p.106 (re 1 Thess. 5.15: 'The parallelism is so close (see also 1 Pet. 3.9)] that the apostle may be dependent on a catechetical tradition akin to that behind Mt. 5.38-39, 44, and Lk. 6.29, 35'); C. E. B. Cranfield, *The Epistle to the Romans*, International Critical Commentary (T & T Clark, Edinburgh, 1979) 2 p.645 (cf Rom. 12.17 with 1 Thess. 5.15. and 1 Pet. 3.9: 'The close similarity between [these passages] ... suggests that we have here the fixed formulation of the catechetical tradition.')

life and expressed solidarity with their neighbours. If they had not done so, to some extent they risked extinction through incomprehensibility.[1] Nevertheless, as Eduardo Hoornaert has seen so well from his Brazilian perspective, joining the Christian community meant being 'converted to marginality.'[2] The word that the early Christians repeatedly adopted for themselves was a socio-legal term: *paroikoi*—'resident aliens'.[3] At home everywhere; fully at home nowhere: the Christians believed that, because of their life in Christ, they were living in a distinctive way that had global and salvation-historical import. There was something catholic, something universal about the life that they shared with others throughout the empire and beyond; and significantly, when under pressure, they often expressed their primary identity in a simple affirmation of allegiance to Christ: 'I am a Christian.'[4] Tertullian also saw the global dimensions of the Christians' allegiance: 'One state we know, of which we are all citizens—the universe.'[5] This vision of global peace, rooted in the peacemaking of Christ Jesus and the enemy-loving of his disciples, underlay the Old Testament passage which was apparently quoted more frequently than any other by the early communities—the swords into ploughshares passage of Isaiah 2.2-4 and Micah 4.1-4.[6] This, many writers believed, had been fulfilled in Christ's world-wide church, and it was the culmination of the Jewish hope.[7] The sheer largeness of this vision was bracing. God was saving individuals, to be sure, but as a part of his grand design for 'the reconciliation and restoration of the human race.'[8] Small wonder that these Christian communities, which appeared to be so marginal, had a self-confidence that was attractive. They believed that they were the instruments that God was using to construct a new world.

---

[1] Anton Wessels, *Europe: Was it Ever Really Christian?* (SCM, London, 1994) ch. 2; Horst Rzep-kowski, 'Das Papsttum als ein Modell frühchristlicher Anpassung,' in Theo Sundermeier (ed.) *Die Begegnung mit dem Anderen: Plädoyers für eine interkulturelle Hermeneutik*, Studiem zum Verstehen fremder Religionen, 2 (Gerd Mohn, Gütersloh, 1991) pp.69-93.

[2] Eduardo Hoornaert, *The Memory of the Christian People*, transl. by R. R. Barr (Orbis Books, Maryknoll, NY, 1988) p.81.

[3] The use of this term, which first appears in Christian use in 1 Peter 2.11, has been carefully studied by Pierre de Labriolle, 'Paroecia' in *Bulletin du Cange* (Archivum Latinitatis Medii Aevi) 3 (1927) pp.196-199. He comments (p.198): 'The idea of the heterogeneity of the Christians from their pagan neighbours and the society where they live is one of those which one finds most frequently in the texts.' For other samples, see 1 Clement, preface; Polycarp, *Phil* preface; 2 Clement, *Ep* 5.1; Eusebius, *HE* 5.1.3; *Epistle to Diognetus* 5.5; Pontius, *Vita Cypriani* II. As J. H. Elliott has demonstrated, the word *paroikos* could have legal and social as well as theological significance for the early Christians (*A Home for the Homeless* (SCM, London, 1981) p.48).

[4] Eusebius, *HE* 5.1.19, 20; *Passio Sanctorum Scillitanorum* (H. Musurillo [ed.] *The Acts of the Christian Martyrs* (Clarendon Press, Oxford, 1972) p.89). For the centrality of Christ in the identity formation of the early Christians, see J. N. Bremmer, ' "Christianus sum:" The Early Christian Martyrs and Christ,' in G. J. M. Bartelink, A. Hilhorst and C. J. Kneepkens (eds.), *Eulogia: Mélanges offert à A. A. R. Bastiaensen à l'occasion de son soixante-cinquième anniversaire*, Instrumenta Patristica, 24 (Nijhoff International, Steenbrugge and the Hague, 1991) pp.11-20.

[5] Tertullian, *Apol* 38.3.

[6] Gerhard Lohfink, ' "Schwerter zu Pflugscharen": Die Rezeption von Jes 2, 1-5 par Mi 4, 1-5 in der Alten Kirche und im Neuen Testament' in *Theologische Quartalschrift* 166 (1986) pp.184-209.

[7] For a partial list, see Justin, *Dial* 109, 110.3; 1 *Apol* 39.1-3; Irenaeus, *Adversus Haereses* 4.34.4; Tertullian, *Adv Iud* 3; *idem*, *Adv Marc* 3.21; 4.1; Origen, *Contra Celsum* 5.33; Cyprian, *De Habitu Virginum* 3; Pseudo-Cyprian, *Adv Iud* 3.

[8] Justin, 1 *Apol* 23.

6. Learning About the 'New World'

How did people learn about that new world? An initial encounter at times came by means of martyrdom, which brought these communities a notoriety that they would have preferred to avoid. The martyrs' endurance in the amphitheatre, while being attacked by starved bears or roasted on chairs of molten iron, was medically inexplicable; their love for each other and their egalitarianism—manifested, for example, by giving the kiss of peace before being despatched by their executioners—was transparent.[1] Those who guarded them reported in admiration that 'there is a power' among them.[2] And the whole process, for those who had never previously given a thought to Christianity, was question-posing. 'What profit has their religion brought them, which they have preferred to their own life?' asked the incredulous onlookers in the Lyons pogrom.[3] Repeatedly the Christians reported that the fidelity of the martyrs had been one of the first things that had attracted their attention to the faith. As Tertullian put it, faithfulness in public suffering 'is the bait that wins people for our school.'[4]

Others learned about the new world in less dramatic ways. It could happen at work, for example through a new worker who was employed in one's workshop who remarked quietly that his community 'alone . . . know the right way to live'; to people who were aware that nothing was going right for them this could be not offensive but intriguing.[5] A number of sources speak of the unobtrusive ministry of itinerants, whether self-conscious missionaries or simply Christians whose jobs took them to new places. Or one could learn about Christianity in the apartment building or neighbourhood where one lived.[6] 'Most converts,' E. Glenn Hinson has observed, 'became acquainted with it through casual contact.'[7] Christians lived scattered throughout the populace, as neighbours. Like countless others they would climb and descend the long flights of stairs in an urban *insula*. Since Christians looked and dressed like everyone else, people would often be surprised to learn that such ordinary people belonged to this extraordinary group.[8] ' "A good man," they say, "this Caius Seius, only that he is a Christian." '[9] As these Christians formed relationships with their neighbours they at times talked about their faith. The pagan Caecilius reported, with distaste, that the Christians were 'silent in public, chattering in corners.'[10] In times of illness or crisis their neighbours, who were learning to trust them, felt increasingly free to turn to Christians, who could offer material help or prayer for healing and release. Many pagans sensed themselves to be bound, comprehensively un-free, the victims of social and spiritual forces much larger

---

[1] Eusebius, *HE* 5.1.52-56; *Passio Perpetuae* 21 (Musurillo, p.131).
[2] *Passio Perpetuae* 9 (Musurillo, *Acts* p.117).
[3] Eusebius, *HE* 5.1.60.
[4] Tertullian, *Apol* 50.13.
[5] Celsus, in Origen, *Contra Celsum* 3.55.
[6] For an interesting example, see John Barns and Henry Chadwick, 'A Letter Ascribed to Peter of Alexandria' in *Journal of Theological Studies*, n.s., 24 (1973) pp.443-455.
[7] E. Glenn Hinson, *The Evangelization of the Roman Empire: Identity and Adaptability* (Mercer University Press, Macon, GA, 1981) p.49; Everett Ferguson, 'Some Factors in the Growth of the Early Church' in *Restoration Quarterly* 16 (1973) p.45.
[8] *Epistle to Diognetus* 5.
[9] Tertullian, *Apol* 3.1
[10] Minucius Felix, *Octavius* 8.4.

than themselves. Christians, by offering the services of exorcists, could help free people not only from 'wild attacks' but from the 'delusions' and 'illusions' of demonic forces.[1] Early Christians such as Irenaeus pointed to the evangelistic function of exorcism: 'Those who have been cleansed often both believe [in Christ] and join themselves to the Church.'[2] And if Christianity spread through these exorcisms it was because, in an age of competitive miracle-working, the Christian God seemed stronger than other gods.[3]

---

[1] Athenagoras, *Legatio* 23.
[2] Irenaeus, *Adversus Haereses* 2.32.4. Other passages which relate exorcism to conversion are Tertullian, *Ad Scapulam* 4; Tertullian, *Apol* 23.18; *Acts of Thomas* 20; Pseudo-Clement, *De Virginitate* 1.10; Minucius Felix, *Octavius* 27.5-7; Origen, *Homilies on Samuel* 1.10; Origen, *Contra Celsum* 7.18; Lactantius, *Div Inst* 5.24; *Apostolic Constitutions* 8.1. Cf. the judgement of Everett Ferguson (*Demonology in the Early Christian World*, Symposium Series, 12 (Edwin Mellen Press, New York, 1984) p.129): '. . . an important factor in the Christian success in the Roman world was the promise which it made of deliverance from demons.'
[3] On the role of miracle in conversion, see the debate between MacMullen, who contends that '*That* was what produced converts. Nothing else is attested' (*Paganism in the Roman Empire* (Yale University Press, New Haven, 1981) p.96), and Lane Fox, who knows of 'no historical case when a miracle or an exorcism turned an individual, let alone a crowd, to the Christian faith' (*Pagans and Christians*, p.330). Lane Fox, in view of the testimony of contemporaries in note 2 above, overlooks the extent to which contemporaries felt that miracle was a component in conversion. MacMullen, on the other hand, engagingly overstates his case, not least because of the (over?) seriousness with which he takes the reports of miracles in the mid-third-century ministry of Gregory [Thaumaturgus] in Pontus. It is fascinating to compare the accounts of two contemporary leaders' strategies for dealing with the plague: that of Gregory, who is said to have combated disease by the miraculous power of his presence, and that of Cyprian (who of course believed in miracle), who urged the Carthaginian Christians to stay in the plague-ridden city and nurse the infected. For Gregory, see Gregory of Nyssa, *Life of Gregory*; Victor Ryssel, *Eine syrische Lebensgeschichte des Gregorius Thaumaturgus* (August Frick, Zürich, 1894); for Cyprian, see Pontius, *Vita Cypriani* 9; Cyprian, *De Mortalitate* 14, 16.

7. Liberation from Bondage

Not only stronger but more profound. Some people in the early centuries were aware that they were indeed oppressed by demons, but that this oppression had social dimensions. The form that this oppression took was at times what we might today call addiction or compulsion. To be 'liberated from bondage' meant to be freed from the sway of the evil one who 'dominated the whole earth.'[1] It was the catechist Justin in Rome, writing around 150, who articulated this most clearly. No doubt reflecting the experience of his students, Justin was acutely aware of the work of the demons, 'who struggle to have you as their slaves and servants.' But, he reported, Christians 'after being persuaded by the Word' have renounced the demons. Through God in Jesus Christ they are now experiencing freedom, in four areas of their lives. Those people, he said, who had been addicted to sexual adventure now 'delight in continence alone.' Those who had been addicted to the magic arts now 'have dedicated themselves to the good and unbegotten God.' Justin then changed from speaking about 'those' to 'we', indicating that he was now speaking about compulsions general to the society against which he and *all* Christians had to struggle.

> '*We* who once took most pleasure in the means of increasing our wealth and property now bring what we have into a common fund and share with everyone in need; *we* who hated and killed one another and would not associate with people of different tribes because of [their different] customs, now after the manifestation of Christ live together and pray for our enemies . . . so that they, living according to the fair commands of Christ, may share with *us* the good hope of receiving the same thing.'[2]

Common to all the inhabitants of Rome, Justin knew, were the addictions of escalating living standards and xenophobic violence. But Christ was liberator: 'His sayings were short and concise, for he was no sophist, but his word was the power of God.'[3] Christ's work on the cross, Justin was convinced, had led to 'the destruction of the demons'[4]; and his teaching had led to the freeing of people in areas in which they were addicted and in bondage.

A good example of a person who experienced this freedom is Cyprian. Cyprian was a patrician Carthaginian whose future as a rhetorician seemed clear. By his early adulthood his reputation was formidable, and his lifestyle was characteristic of his class. But Cyprian was dissatisfied. He sensed himself powerless in the face of powers that were larger than he was—the 'corruption of our own material nature,' the habits and assumptions that are 'deeply and radically engrained in us.' What was the particular point of bondage, or addiction, for Cyprian? It was the patterns of accumulation, consumption and rank differentiation characteristic of his social station. 'When,' he agonized,

> 'does a person learn thrift who has been used to liberal banquets and sumptuous feasts? And a person who has been glittering in gold and purple, and has been celebrated for his costly attire, when does he reduce himself to ordinary and simple

---

[1] Origen, *Contra Celsum* 7.18.
[2] Justin, 1 *Apol* 14 (italics mine).
[3] *Ibid*.
[4] Justin, 2 *Apol* 6.

clothing? One who has felt the charm of the fasces and of civic honours shrinks from becoming a mere private and inglorious citizen. The man who is attended by crowds of clients, and dignified by the numerous association of an officious train, regards it as a punishment when he is alone.'[1]

How does one break free of these compulsions? Cyprian, his biographer Pontius reported, had a 'close association' with Caecilius, a 'just man'. This Christian elder became 'the friend and comrade of his soul' and apparently functioned as his sponsor as Cyprian progressed towards membership in the Christian community.[2] There, through a powerful experience (which we shall discuss in a moment), Cyprian, bishop-to-be, martyr-to-be, experienced 'new birth'; and, to his delight, he discovered the freedom which enabled him to 'put off what he has previously been.'[3]

Caecilius's friendship was a vital ingredient in Cyprian's coming to faith and freedom. And throughout the early centuries, there were no doubt countless people who played the role of friend. 'Affective bonds', which sociologists have shown to be central in attracting people to countercultural religious groups, were at play here.[4] Pagans, Justin noted, were turning 'away from the ways of violence and tyranny' because they were drawn to Christians as people whose lives were distinctive, and free. The pagans' hesitations were overcome 'by observing the consistent lives of their neighbours, or noting the strange patience of their injured acquaintances, or experiencing the way they did business with them.'[5] Women apparently were disproportionately involved in forming evangelistically productive 'affective bonds'.[6] This is partly because they were from an early date preponderant numerically in the church.[7] It also reflected their ability to listen to people and to be attentive to their questions.[8] Inevitably, then as now, a major concern of women was the salvation of their husbands, who as a group seem to have

---

[1] These, according to Ramsay MacMullen, were among the classic indicators of the senatorial *ordo*. See his *Corruption and the Decline of Rome* (Yale University Press, New Haven, 1988) pp.62-64.

[2] Did Caecilius represent the same social stratum as Cyprian, and thus represent the recruitment potential of 'preexisting social networks'? See L. Michael White, 'Finding the Ties that Bind: Issues from Social Description' in *Semeia* 56 (1991) p.21.

[3] Cyprian, *Ep* 1, *Ad Donatum* 3-4; Pontius, *Vita Cypriani* 4. In one of his treatises (*De Lapsis* 11) Cyprian interprets those whose 'wealth fettered them like a chain' as those who are in spiritual bondage—'booty and food for the serpent.'

[4] John Lofland and Rodney Stark, 'Becoming a World-Saver: A Theory of Conversion to a Deviant Perspective' in *American Sociological Review* 30 (1965) p.871.

[5] Justin, 1 *Apol* 16.

[6] Brox, 'Zur christlichen Mission' p.223; John Foster, *After the Apostles: Missionary Preaching in the First Three Centuries* (SCM Press, London, 1951) pp.40, 42.

[7] Lane Fox, *Pagans and Christians* p.310; Harnack, *Mission and Expansion* II p.81. For examples of the evidence, see *Canons of Elvira* 15, which refers to 'the large number of girls'; or the list of clothing at the disposal of the church of Cirta in North Africa in 303, in *Gesta apud Zenophilum, 3*, in Ramsay MacMullen and Eugene N. Lane (eds.) *Paganism and Christianity, 100-425 C.E.: A Sourcebook* (Fortress Press, Minneapolis, 1992) p.249.

[8] *Didascalia Apostolorum* 3.5. The male church leaders, who recognized this gift, seem to have been fearful of it; their greater concern was the 'internal stabilizing and external adaptation' of the congregation (Rosemarie Nürnberg, ' "Non decet neque necessarium est, ut mulieres doceant": Ueberlegungen zum altkirchlichen Lehrverbot für Frauen' in *Jahrbuch für Antike und Christentum* 31 (1988) p.66.

been more locked in paganism than they were.[1] These pre-Christendom patterns were still evident in the time of Augustine, over a century after the conversion of Constantine: 'O you men,' he wrote, 'who all fear the burden imposed by baptism. You are easily beaten by your women. Chaste and devoted to the faith, it is their presence in great numbers that causes the church to grow.'[2] Whether with women or with men, it was friendship which was the most common way for individuals to approach the seemingly unapproachable Christian churches.

---

[1] Tertullian, *Ad Uxorem* 2.7; *Apostolic Constitutions* 1.10.
[3] Augustine to Firmus, *Ep* 2*.4.1-7 (Divjak), q. Peter Brown, *The Body and Society: Men, Women and Sexual Renunciation in Early Christianity* (Faber and Faber, London, 1989) p.342. Kate Cooper has argued that this kind of argument can reveal more about the rhetoric of power struggle among competitive groups of men than about the evangelistic activities of women ('Insinuations of Womanly Influence: An Aspect of the Christianization of the Roman Aristocracy' in *Journal of Roman Studies* 82 (1992) pp.150-164.

8. A Socially-Inclusive Community

There was yet another way: the way of community. Just as individual Christians were quietly conspicuous for their freedom, so also entire Christian communities were evident as communities of freedom. Outsiders often misconstrued what was going on in the churches. As the pagan Caecilius commented:

'[The Christians] are a gang of discredited and proscribed desperadoes ... They have gathered together from the lowest dregs of the populace ignorant men and credulous women—and women are naturally unstable—and have formed a rabble of impious conspirators ... they fall in love almost before they are acquainted; everywhere they introduce a kind of religion of lust ...'[1]

Caecilius's was a somewhat uncharitable view, of course, but he was not unperceptive. He noted the preponderance of women, which we have already observed, and of 'ignorant' people evidently from the lower social orders. But by addressing his complaints to Octavius, a highly literate non-plebeian believer, Caecilius was conceding that the Christian churches were socially inclusive to an extent unparalleled in ancient society. After much debate, scholars in recent years have been coming to much the same conclusion. According to Professor Peter Lampe of the University of Kiel, who has done a wide-ranging study of the churches in urban Rome in the first two centuries, 'Christianity more or less mirrored the stratification of the entire society'—except for an absence of patrician males, who of course had the most power to lose. This would mean that there were many more poor people than rich people in the churches in Rome. However, he also noted that among the Christians there was 'an intensive exchange', in which richer Christians gave through the church's common fund to their poorer brothers and sisters, leading to 'a limited material equalization between the strata.'[2] And the equalization was not only material. As Lane Fox commented, 'Christianity made the least-expected social groups articulate'—women, slaves, people who had been discarded as unwanted babies on the local tip.[3] Not everyone was happy about this equalization, to be sure; some people who were becoming rich hesitated to come to the services, where they would as a part of their worship be expected to give generously to the common fund.[4] There was also, as a result of the generosity of the Roman Christians and their remarkable institutions for mutual aid and poor relief, a growth in the overall wealth of the Roman church institutions which was eventually to have deleterious effects on the life of the Roman Christians. However, what is notable about the Roman Christians at the time when Caecilius was observing them was their social inclusivity and generosity. Some outsiders were mistrustful of this; others wanted to join it.

---

[1] Minucius Felix, *Octavius* 8.4; 9.2.

[2] Lampe, *Die stadtrömischen Christen* pp.113-114. The objections of Georg Schöllgen ('Probleme der frühchristlichen Sozialgeschichte: Einwände gegen Peter Lampes Buch' in *Jahrbuch für Antike und Christentum* 32 (1989) pp.23-40) are not sufficient to detract from Lampe's overall conclusions. For a similar equalization in churches far from Rome, see L. William Countryman, 'Welfare in the Churches of Asia Minor under the Early Roman Empire' in *Society of Biblical Literature, 1979 Seminar Papers* (Scholars Press, Missoula, Montana, 1979) I pp.143-144; and Carole E. Straw, 'Cyprian and Mt. 5.45: the Evolution of Christian Patronage' in *Studia Patristica* 18, 3 (1989) p.335.

[3] Lane Fox, *Pagans and Christians* p.330. The father of a reader in an Egyptian church in 303 was named Copreus, meaning 'off the dung heap' (*ibid*. p.282).

[4] Hermas, *Sim* 9.20.2; *Didascalia Apostolorum* 2.61.

9. A Community of Peace

Caecilius's second observation was also shrewd. For the Christians did indeed view themselves as brothers and sisters, members of the same family, bound together in the love and peace of Christ. From the outset, being a people of peace had required tending. Even Clement's first letter, customarily viewed as an appeal to the Corinthians to restore a hierarchical view of the church, was rather above all an expression of 'the conviction that the Christians form a common *adelphotes* which must be preserved' through reciprocal humility and service.[1] In time, the Christian communities developed means of tending this corporateness, both through the disciplines of inter-communal reconciliation and through a ritual observance—the kiss of peace—which expressed both the love that bound them to each other as well as their equality in Christ.[2] This rite, even more than the social inclusiveness of the Christians, lent itself to misinterpretation by unsympathetic onlookers, who could generalize upon rumours of unbridled sexual behaviour on the part of certain gnostic groups.[3] For good reason the Christians in Athens had a communal rule which forbade anyone to kiss twice 'because it was pleasurable.'[4] But the early Christians knew that central to their communities' life was a peace that was unworldly and deeply attractive.

The Christians were aware that the life of their communities was remarkable; and they wanted to live in such a way that this was visible enough to draw people to faith and freedom in Christ. 'Beauty of life,' one of them contended, ' . . . causes strangers to join the ranks . . . We do not talk about great things; we live them.'[5] A strenuous communal lifestyle required constant pastoral supervision; and it is likely that the clergy gave their primary attention not to evangelism but to the church's inner life precisely because of their 'confidence that the clearly and distinctively lived ideal will most effectively make people attentive to the truth of Christianity.'[6] The church orders, which attempted to regulate the life of the early communities, exemplify this concern. The *Didascalia Apostolorum* emphasized that by nurturing right relationships within the church Christian leaders would be 'helpers with God that the number of those who are saved may be increased . . .'[7] For this reason, wrangling, enmity and the like were especially to be avoided, 'lest you scatter some one from the Church.' The same concern was evident for the individual believers who had been shaped by the Church's common life and witness. Let us, the *Apostolic Tradition* enjoined, 'compete among the pagans in being like-minded and sober.'[8] And the early fourth-century *Canons of Hippolytus* expressed the desire that the lives of Christians 'may shine with virtue, not before each other [only], but also before the Gentiles so they may imitate them and become Christians . . .'[9]

---

[1] Barbara Ellen Bowe, *A Church in Crisis: Ecclesiology and Paraenesis in Clement of Rome*, Harvard Dissertations in Religion, 23 (Fortress Press, Minneapolis, 1988) pp.4, 155.

[2] 'It was proper to offer a kiss of greeting, to the hem of the emperor's robe, to a knee, to a hand. Equals kissed on the level.' (MacMullen, *Corruption and the Decline of Rome* p.63).

[3] For example, Epiphanius, *Panarion* 26.4-5. Cf. Sephen Benko, 'The Libertine Gnostic Sect of the Phibionites according to Epiphanius' in *Vigiliae Christianae* 21 (1967) pp.103-119.

[4] Athenagoras, *Legatio* 32.

[5] Minucius Felix, *Octavius* 31.7; 38.5.

[6] Brox, 'Zur christlichen Mission' p.211.

[7] *Didascalia Apostolorum* 2.54; cf. *Apostolic Constitutions* 4.54.

[8] *Apostolic Tradition* 29.

[9] *Canons of Hippolytus* 19.

10. Witness through Mercy

So these communities were by no means ingrown. Among their activities often were means of serving the material needs of their neighbours which dumbfounded the imagination of their contemporaries. For example, the Christians in Alexandria intervened, on both sides, in a civil war to attempt to mediate a dispute and to bring relief to both parties; the Christians in Carthage nursed the pagan victims of the terrible plague of 252.[1] In many places the Christians provided hospitality and poor relief to pagans as well as believers. The sincerest flattery of this came from the ex-Christian emperor Julian, who in the 360s was finding it difficult to reinstitute paganism as the religion of the Roman Empire. The problem, he discovered, was that the Christians had been so generous. He bewailed: '. . . it is their benevolence to strangers, their care for the graves of the dead and the pretended holiness of their lives that have done most to increase their atheism . . . the impious Galileans support not only their own poor but ours as well.' However, Julian's attempts to get the pagan priests to stir their adherents to comparable practices were, like his brief reign, barren. For all his contention that 'this was our practice of old,' nobody believed him. The pagans had neither the living traditions, nor the theological understandings, nor the communal disciplines, nor the appropriate rites, to make this practice live among them.[2]

But live it did among the Christians. A telling example comes from upper Egypt, in the period just prior to the conversion of Emperor Constantine. In 312 the local imperial forces, sensing the need to replenish the legions, conscripted some young men and shipped them, guarded by soldiers, down the Nile to Thebes. There, to prevent the conscripts escaping, they were held in a prison. 'In the evening some merciful Christians, hearing about them, brought them something to eat and drink and other necessities, because they were in distress.' One of the conscripts, twenty-year-old Pachomius, asked who these merciful people were. He was told that they were Christians, and that 'Christians were merciful to everyone, including strangers.' But, he repeated, what is a Christian? ' "They are people who bear the name of Christ, the only begotten Son of God, and they do good to everyone, putting their hope in him who made heaven and earth and us people." Hearing of this great grace,' the account continues, '[Pachomius's] heart was set on fire with the fear of God and with joy. Withdrawing alone in the prison, he raised his hands to heaven' and offered himself in love for God and the service of others. Shortly thereafter, after being discharged, Pachomius went to a nearby village where he was instructed and baptized. Through the active mercy of a local community of Christians, Pachomius, the organizing genius of early conventual monasticism, was won for the faith.[3] Pachomius's was not an exceptional conversion; nor was it simply the result of 'the practical application of charity.'[4] It was the natural product of a community whose common life was animated by deviant values—and was actively attractive.

---

[1] Eusebius, *HE* 7.32.7-12; Pontius, *Vita Cypriani* 9. For comment, see Kretschmar, 'Das christliche Leben' p.124; Rodney Stark, 'Epidemics, Networks, and the Rise of Christianity,' *Semeia* 56 (1992) pp.159-175.

[2] Julian, *Ep* 22 (MacMullen and Lane, *Paganism and Christianity* pp.270-271).

[3] 'The First Greek Life of Pachomius' in Armand Veilleux (ed) *Pachomian Koinonia*, I: *The Life of Saint Pachomius and his Disciples* (Cistercian Publications, Kalamazoo, MI, 1980) pp.300-301.

[4] Henry Chadwick, *The Early Church* (Penguin Books, Harmondsworth, Middx. 1967) p.56; cf. Kretschmar, 'Das christliche Leben' p.120.

But how was it that Christians were able to behave like this? Here I come to the heart of the matter. I am convinced that the secret was in their worship, which above all shaped individuals and communities that were distinctive. But before one could worship one had to get through the doors of the church. And that, as we have noted, was not easy.

11. Catechism: Constructing the 'New World'

There was a brief period in the first century in which baptism seemed to follow almost immediately upon confession of Jesus as Lord (Acts 2.38; 8.26-40; 16.33). But by the second century churches all over the empire had slowed down greatly the process of baptismal preparation. (There was also, in many churches, at least from the second century, the practice of infant baptism, but the language and shape of the baptismal rite shows that adult baptism remained the main route of entry to the church up to the fifth century).[1] The early converts to the messianic faith who were baptized quickly had been largely either Jews or god-fearers, who would be steeped in the Hebrew scriptures and way of life. By the second century, however, converts, coming to Christianity directly from a variety of paganisms, were ignorant of these.[2] Their lives and outlooks represented a late Roman cultural consensus which Christian thinkers viewed as a form of bondage. 'Captives we have been,' Origen declared, 'who for many years Satan held in bonds.'[3] This captivity had been to idols, but also to 'this worship, more subtle than that of idols, which is greed.'[4] Such bondage needed to be broken, and a period of catechism culminating in baptism was the means by which the Church attempted to ensure that its members were free people.[5]

As always, friendship was the way to approach the church. In the early period the befriending believers themselves may have been the ones to catechize potential

---

[1] Joseph Lynch, *Godparents and Kinship in Early Medieval Europe* (Princeton University Press, 1986) p.120. For recent discussion of the origins of infant baptism see Everett Ferguson, 'Inscriptions and the Origin of Infant Baptism' in *Journal of Theological Studies* n.s. 30 (1979) pp.37-46; David F. Wright, 'How Controversial Was the Development of Infant Baptism in the Early Church?' in J. E. Bradley and R. A. Muller (eds.), *Church, Word and Spirit: Historical and Theological Essays in Honor of Geoffrey W. Bromiley* (Eerdmans, Grand Rapids, 1987) pp.45-63; *idem*, 'The Origins of Infant Baptism—Child Believers' Baptism?' in *Scottish Journal of Theology* 40 (1987) pp.1-23; *idem*, 'One Baptism or Two? Reflections on the History of Christian Baptism' in *Vox Evangelica* 18 (1988) pp.7-23.

[2] Lynch, *Godparents and Kinship* p.86.

[3] Origen, *Homilies on Luke* 32.4.

[4] Origen, *Homilies on Joshua* 1.7.

[5] A further concern of the Christian leaders was that potential baptismal candidates might have been infected by one or more heresies that were circulating in the Christian world. For a discussion of the deferring of baptism, see Lynch, *Godparents and Kinship* p.87.

Christians.[1] Or a person exploring the faith might wish to attend a school such as Justin's in Rome.[2] But by the later second century in many parts of the empire a pattern of formal catechism had developed.[3] Believers who had befriended pagans, when convinced of their seriousness, would bring them, early in the morning before one of the church's daily meetings, to speak with a catechist. This teacher, according to the third-century *Apostolic Tradition*, would question both the sponsors and the potential candidates.[4] What is the marital state of the candidates? If the candidates are slaves, what do their masters think? Are the candidates involved in some profession, such as charioteering or sculpting images, that the church utterly rejects? 'Let him cease or be rejected.' If the candidate is in a difficult profession, such as military service, they may be catechized only if they promise not to kill. If they kill, or if one of them as a catechumen joins the legions, 'let him be rejected.'[5] This inquiry stage has been called, by liturgical theologian Robert Webber, a 'weeding-out process.'[6] It may seem perverse to reject people before one has taught them, but that was not how the early Christians saw things. Their concern rather was to maintain and nurture the character of the community, in the face of a hostile surrounding society. Conversion, they believed, began less at the level of belief than at the level of lifestyle. Only a person who was willing to change his or her 'conduct and his habits' was someone who was 'capable of hearing the word.'[7]

Thereafter began a process which could take up to three years of catechism (although 'if a man is keen . . . the time shall not be judged, but only his conduct').[8] During this period, in some areas every single morning before going to work, the catechumens would come to the church house for an hour of study. At times their sponsors would accompany them, and other believers would generally also be there. They would hear a reading from the Bible; they would listen to an address by a catechist, who often

---

[1] Michael Gärtner, *Die Familienerziehung in der alten Kirche*, Kölner Veröffentlichungen zur Religionsgeschichte, 7 (Böhlau Verlag, Cologne, 1985) p.80.

[2] Lampe, *Die stadtrömischen Christen* p.299, views the lectures of Justin and Valentinus as a separate category from the catechism which had been provided either in the *oikos* or the formal catechetical instructions as described in *AT*. From Justin's *Acta* 3 (Musurillo, *Acts* p.45) it appears that 'anyone who wished' could come to his school, which would not be characteristic of the carefully screened entrance to the church's formal catecheses. On the other hand, he reports (*Apol* 61) that 'those who are persuaded and believe that the things we teach and say are true, and promise that they can live accordingly,' are allowed into the final preprations for baptism, while Justin prays and fasts along with them. Justin may best be viewed, therefore, as a teacher who serves both as catechist and befriending sponsor. Cf. Ulrich Neymeyr, *Die christlichen Lehrer im zweiten Jahrhundert: Ihre Lehrtätigkeit, ihre Selbstverständnis und ihre Geschichte*, Supplements *Vigiliae Christianae*, 4 (Brill, Leiden, 1989) pp.33, 35, who views Justin as a 'pneumatic teacher,' a 'philosophical teacher,' and a 'missionary teacher.'

[3] A. Hamman, 'Catechumen, Catechumenate,' in Angelo di Berardino (ed.), *Encyclopedia of the Early Church* (James Clarke, Cambridge, 1992) I p.151.

[4] Recent scholarship has called into question the customary authorship (Hippolytus) and place of origin (Rome) of the *Apostolic Tradition*; as yet no 'new orthodoxy' has arisen to replace the old. See Paul Bradshaw, *The Search for the Origins of Christian Worship* (SPCK, London, 1992) pp.89-92; Marcel Metzger, 'Enquêtes autour de la prétendue "Tradition Apostolique" ' in *Ecclesia Orans* 9 (1992) pp.22-30.

[5] *Apostolic Tradition* 15-16.

[6] Robert Webber, 'Ethics and Evangelism: Learning from the Third-Century Church ' in *Christian Century* (24 September 1986) p.806.

[7] Origen, *Homilies on Luke* 22.5; *Apostolic Tradition* 15.

[8] *Apostolic Tradition* 17. Cf. Canon 11 of the early fourth-century Canons of Elvira, which refer to a five-year catechumenate.

exposited the Biblical passage which had been read, and which they might, in dialogical fashion, interrupt; there would be a prayer, and the catechumens would depart after having received a blessing.[1]

What did they learn in these sessions? Scholars have, in rather tedious fashion, spoken of doctrinal, moral, and liturgical materials; but they have generally done this without considering the pastoral purpose of the catechism. This, I believe, was to re-form pagan people, to resocialize them, to deconstruct their old world, and reconstruct a new one, so that they would emerge as Christian people who would be at home in communities of freedom. And to help the catechumens progress on this journey, the catechists needed especially to instruct the them in two areas essential to the life of any community: history and folkways.

---

[1] The basis for the material in this paragraph, largely drawn from the *Apostolic Tradition* and from Origen's daily catecheses in Caesarea between 239-242, is the work of Pierre Nautin: his introduction to Origen, *Homélies sur Jérémie*, Sources chrétiennes, 232 (Cerf, Paris, 1976) pp.100-112; and his *Origène: Sa vie et son oeuvre*, Christianisme Antique, 1 (Beauchesne, Paris, 1977) pp.391-407. Some of Nautin's reconstructions, for example of three-year lectionary/ catechetical cycles, though immensely learned, seem a little too ingenious. Nautin also, in my view, misses the point of catechism, which was not just to cover the Bible ('The preaching which they heard in the assemblies served them as catechism.' *Homélies sur Jérémie* p.110) but to prepare the catechumens to be members of communities whose life and witness took place in potentially dangerous circumstances.

12. A New History

The first of these, as Professor Everett Ferguson has recently pointed out, is the primary means by which any community develops its sense of identity.[1] The stories that people tell, and the history that they remember, the heroes and heroines whom they venerate, all shape a community's consciousness. The typical pagan entering Christian catechism had a mental melange of historical data—myths about gods, national exploits, local heroes. To enable the catechumen to become ready to join the Christian community, the catechist needed to replace this mythico-historical mix by an alternative narrative, by the history of salvation as recounted in the books of the Hebrew Scriptures which culminated in the person and work of Jesus Christ and which continued in the life of the transnational church and the sufferings of the martyrs. In Ferguson's view, 'The Old Testament was more than an explication and proof of the New Testament message; as the story of God's saving deeds it was the very framework of catechesis and provided the setting for presenting Christ, the very centre of that catechesis.'[2] Convincingly Ferguson argues that Irenaeus's *Proof of the Apostolic Preaching* is a catechetical document designed to impart a living narrative to catechumens.[3] And, if conceived in this light, it even makes sense that Origen's daily Old Testament expositions can be seen as catechetical. He was providing for his hearers a living history which, by superseding their old history, would equip them to respond to the life situations they would encounter with precedents that were life-giving.

---

[1] Everett Ferguson, 'Irenaeus' Proof of the Apostolic Preaching and Early Catechetical Tradition' in *Studia Patristica* 18, 3 (1989) pp.119-140.
[2] *Ibid*. 134.
[3] E.g., Egeria, *Travels* 46.2-3; Augustine, *De Cat Rud* 1.3, 6; 2.18-24, 26-27.

13. New Folkways

The second essential area covered by the catechists had to do with folkways. I use this term rather than 'ethics' or 'morality' because it has to do with the ways of a people which are often assumed rather than consciously thought out; they are habitual, even reflexive.[1] The pagans undergoing catechism needed to be *rehabituated* so that they would react to situations of tension and difficulty in a distinctive way, not like pagans, but like members of a Christian community, and ideally like Jesus. At the heart of the imparting of folkways, as Origen pointed out, was imitation: hence the importance of the life example on the part of catechists and sponsors alike.[2]

But the catechists also taught folkways by precept. From the end of the first century Christian writers divided approaches to life according to 'two ways, one of life and one of death.'[3] Subsequent Christian writers referred to the 'teaching' which their communities imparted. They had to prepare their catechumens, for example, to face martyrdom; or to know how to behave in public bath-houses; or how to avoid swearing oaths; or how to respond to enemies and warfare.[4] One document, Cyprian's *Ad Quirinum* book 3, provides a full agenda for 'the religious teaching of our school', providing copious biblical citations for 120 'precepts of the Lord.' First on his list and much the longest, as we might expect in light of Cyprian's pre-baptismal struggle with materialism, was 'of the benefit of good works and mercy,' for which he provided no fewer than 36 biblical texts. Other precepts had to do with peaceful living together in the Christian community, with relations to the 'Gentile' world, and rather unpopularly today with 'the benefit of virginity and continence'.[5] As a quick perusal of Cyprian's biblical texts will indicate, at the heart of his entire teaching, and I believe of the inculcation of early Christian folkways by many catechists, was the person and teaching of Jesus Christ. Athenagoras: 'What then are the teachings on which we are brought up? "I say to you, love them who curse you, pray for them who persecute you, that you may be the sons of your Father in heaven." '[6] Aristeides: 'Now the Christians . . . have the commandments of the Lord Jesus Christ himself engraven on their hearts, and these they observe.'[7] And Justin, catechizing in Rome, was intensely aware that he was a mediator of the Jesus tradition: as recipient of 'teachings which have come from Christ himself,' he sought to 'teach these things truly' to others.[8]

During this period, possibly several years in length, while the catechumens were internalizing the history of God's people and experiencing a re-reflexing of their responses, they also participated in the first part of the Sunday worship of the church. Week after week they entered the door, but only just. For, although on Sundays as other days they heard the reading of the Scriptures and the expositions of the presbyters, they were then reminded that they were only catechumens by being asked to leave before the mysterious rites that followed.[9]

---

[1] Stanley Hauerwas, *The Peaceable Kingdom* (SCM Press, London, 1984) p.125: 'Morally the most important things about us are those matters about which we never have to make a "decision." '

[2] Origen, *Homilies on Jeremiah* 4.6.

[3] *Didache* 1.1; Barnabas, *Ep* 18-21; *Epistula Apostolorum* 37-39; *Passio Perpetuae* 4; Lactantius, *Div Inst* 6.3, *Epitome* 59; and, with a new twist, Eusebius, *Dem Ev* 1.8.

[4] *Didascalia Apostolorum* 5.5; Epiphanius, *Panarion* 30.7; John Chrysostom, *Baptismal Instructions* (ed. P. W. Harkins) pp.143-146, 155-160; Origen, *Contra Celsum* 3.8; *idem, Homilies on Joshua* 15.1.

[5] Cyprian, *Ad Quirinum* 3.1-2 (good works and wealth); living in peaceful community (3, 8, 9, 21, 22, 109, 113); relations with outsiders (34, 44, 62); virginity and continence (32).

[6] Athenagoras, *Legatio* 11.2.

[7] Aristeides, *Apol* 15.

[8] Justin, 1 *Apol* 14.

[9] *Apostolic Tradition* 18-19.

14. Baptism: 'Singing a New Song'

But at some point, often in the weeks prior to Easter, the catechumens, accompanied by their sponsors, were called before the church leaders to be scrutinized for their suitability for membership in the Christian community. The questions which they and their sponsors were asked did not have to do with their doctrinal comprehension; they rather had to do with folkways. 'Let their life be examined,' the *Apostolic Tradition* enjoins. 'Have they lived good lives when they were catechumens? Have they honoured the widows? Have they visited the sick? Have they done every kind of good work?'[1] The *Canons of Hippolytus* sharpen the question to the candidate. 'Are you in two minds, or under pressure from anything, or driven by convention?'[2] Had the candidates, in short, been living like Christians? Were they ready to live like Christians? If so, they were then ready to enter into the most strenuous period of their entire pre-baptismal preparation.

Every day during the weeks before their baptism at Easter they were to 'hear the gospel', that is be taught the 'rule of faith' which provided a doctrinal framework for their life and understandings.[3] Daily they also had hands laid on them by the church leaders, who exorcised all lurkings of 'the Alien' from them. This, according to William Willimon, served as a final 'detoxification of the dominant order.'[4] In the days immediately before Easter they fasted, received further exorcisms, and on Easter Eve they held an all-night vigil. The climax of this process came at cockcrow on Easter morning. The water in the baptistry was blessed. And then, as the *Apostolic Tradition* calmly puts it, 'They shall take off their clothes.' Divested of the old, vulnerable, naked, the catechumens went down into the water and, after being baptized in the name of the Father, the Son and the Holy Spirit, they, having died to their old selves, emerged as Christians who were alive. They were anointed with the oil of thanksgiving, and, having put on their garments, they went through the door into the church. There for the first time, together with all the people, their new family, they raised their hands in prayer. It was at this point, in Tertullian's community, that the newly-baptized person asked God for the charisms of the Holy Spirit.[5] '. . . [W]hen they have prayed, they shall give the kiss of peace.' And then, for the first time they received the eucharist.[6]

Imagine the emotional impact of these experiences. Margaret Miles of Harvard has written about the the way that they 'realize—make real—in a person's body the strong experiences that, together with the religious community's interpretation of that experience, produced a counter-cultural religious self.'[7] The experience of baptism and

---

[1] *Ibid.* 20. Pontius, *Vita Cypriani* 6, refers to 'the poor, whom [Cyprian] as a catechumen . . . had loved.'

[2] *Canons of Hippolytus* 19.

[3] Although *Apostolic Tradition* 20 does not spell out the content of the teaching when the candidates 'hear the gospel,' fourth-century catechists used this as a period to 'hand over' and expound the Creed.

[4] William H. Willimon, *Peculiar Speech: Preaching to the Baptized* (Eerdmans, Grand Rapids, 1992) p.59.

[5] Tertullian, *On Baptism* 20; for comment, see Metzger, 'Enquêtes' pp.20-21; Kilian McDonnell and George T. Montague, *Christian Initiation and Baptism in the Holy Spirit: Evidence from the First Eight Centuries* (Liturgical Press, Collegeville, MN, 1991) pp.98-105.

[6] *Apostolic Tradition* 21.

[7] Margaret R. Miles, *Carnal Knowing: Female Nakedness and Religious Meaning in the Christian West* (Beacon Press, Boston, 1989) p.24.

the eucharist would be all the more potent because, at least from the beginning of the third century, these were secret rites whose meaning the catechumens were not taught until after they had experienced them. Origen, for example, in full flight in one of his homilies, suddenly got uncharacteristically vague and began talking obscurely about 'these august and sublime mysteries which only those know who have the right to know them.'[1] But now, in a final post-Easter week of catechisms, the new believers learned the symbolism and life significance of what they had already experienced in baptism and eucharist. Not only did they now understand what Christians were doing behind the closed doors; they were now full members of the Christian community.

The early Christian writers, unlike many later ones, were reticent in discussing the affective dimensions of their experience.[3] But occasionally one gets a sense of the release, the liberation which they experienced. Origen assured catechumens that 'you descend into the waters . . . you come up again a "new man", ready to "sing a new song." '[3] Even more telling is Cyprian, who had struggled so much with his inability to live simply. Cyprian reported that the experience of baptism made all the difference. 'By the help of the water of new birth, the stain of former years had been washed away, and a light from above . . . had been infused into my reconciled heart.' At the core of this was the Holy Spirit. 'By the agency of the Spirit breathed from heaven' Cyprian knew that he had become 'a new man.' And this experience transformed his lifestyle. He could live simply, unostentatiously. 'What before had seemed difficult began to suggest a means of accomplishment, what had been thought impossible, to be capable of being achieved.'[4] Now that he was baptized, Cyprian not only had a new label—'Christian'; Cyprian sensed himself to be free.

---

[1] Origen, *Homilies on Joshua* 1.4.
[2] The writers are equally reticent in reporting on the 'charismatic' dimension of their worship. Tertullian speaks (*De Anima* 9.4) of a woman who throughout the various parts of the Montanist liturgy was accustomed to have 'gifts of revelation'. More surprisingly, Origen, in un-Montanist Jerusalem, describes a scene during one of his homilies in which a woman began to cry out and what was evidently an exorcism took place (Origen, *Homilies on Samuel* 1.10). It is not easy to reconstruct the liturgical setting for the prophetic ministry which evidently flourished in much early Christian worship, although Hermas (*Mand* 11.9, 14) seems to indicate that in Rome this took place during the prayers. Cf. Heinrich Kraft, 'Die Lyoner Märtyrer und der Montanismus,' in Ernst Dassmann and K. Suso Frank (eds) *Pietas: Festschrift für Bernhard Kötting* (Aschendorff, Münster, 1980) p.251.
[3] Origen, *Homilies on Exodus* 5.5.
[4] Cyprian, *Ep* 1, *Ad Donatum* 4.

15. Worship that Shapes a Distinctive Common Life

What was it that would keep Cyprian, and his baptized sisters and brothers, free? What was it that would make them into communities of freedom that would communicate good news to the world? It was worship, expressed in a series of practices, performed every Lord's Day in their quasi-domestic meetings. For these practices were important, not only to enable the worshipper to encounter God, but also to shape a distinctive common life that would be visible to the world and attractive to it.

16. The Kiss of Peace: Equalizing and Peacemaking

One of these practices was the 'kiss of peace', which in the Sunday services came after the prayers and before the eucharist. Passages in the writings of Paul and Peter indicate that this was already important in the earliest Christian communities.[1] Why this emphasis upon a such a curious practice? Professor William Klassen has seen this in a 'living context of people who are building a new sociological reality.' They, from many backgrounds, had experienced reconciliation with and through Jesus Christ. From many families, they had become brothers and sisters. 'Such an emerging social reality called for new practices . . . and new forms of greeting.'[2] The holy kiss was thus not simply liturgical gesture; it was an expression of revolutionary social bonding and of 'radical equality'.[3] On public display in the amphitheatre, its demonstrative equalizing must have been scandalous. One can imagine the impact upon the Carthage crowd when in 203 in Carthage the martyrs—all of them catechumens but including the slaves Revocatus and Felicitas as well as Vibia Perpetua 'of noble family and upbringing'—'sealed their martyrdom with the kiss of peace'.[4]

---

[1] Rom. 16.16; 1 Cor. 16.20; 2 Cor. 13.12; 1 Thess. 5.26; 1 Pet. 5.14. Cf. G. J. Cuming, 'Service Endings in the Epistles' in *New Testament Studies* 22 (1976) pp.110-113; *idem*, 'New Testament Foundations for Common Prayer' in *Studia Liturgica* 10 (1974) pp.88-105.

[2] William Klassen, 'The Sacred Kiss in the New Testament: An Example of Social Boundary Lines' in *New Testament Studies* 39 (1993) p.132.

[3] L. Edward Phillips, *The Ritual Kiss in Early Christian Worship* (University of Notre Dame, Ph.D. thesis, 1992) p.271.

[4] *Passio Perpetuae* 2, 22.

This form of greeting, which Christians apparently used on a variety of occasions, became a regular part of the developing rites of Christian worship.[1] By Justin's time it was, in Rome, the regular means of ending the service of the word before the eucharist began.[2] And it was practised not just in Rome but in North Africa and the East as well. There were, of course, occasionally problems connected with this, as in Alexandria where some Christians, according to Clement, were neglecting to kiss 'with a chaste and closed mouth'.[3] Despite the possibility of abuse by insiders and misinterpretation by outsiders, the kiss was an essential part of early worship. Not only did it celebrate and communicate the presence of the Spirit in the church[4]; it also provided a means of making peace and effecting unity, thereby safeguarding and, if necessary, restoring the distinctive quality of relationships among the believers. And without this, they believed, their prayers and eucharist would be null and void.

Already in the *Didache* we observe this theme: 'Anyone at variance with his neighbour must not join you, until they are reconciled, lest your sacrifice be defiled.'[5] Tertullian, justifying his view in the classical dominical text (Matthew 5.23-24), urged 'that we not go up to God's altar before we compose whatever of discord or offence we have contracted with our brethren.'[6] During the third and fourth centuries Christian writers repeatedly appealed to this text as they admonished their people.[7] In the fourth century it was often 'the church herald, that is to say, the deacon' who enunciated the liturgical summons to unity. And repeatedly the liturgical documents justify the deacon's invitation to the people to 'Greet one another with the holy kiss' by citing Jesus' Sermon on the Mount injunction.[8] In a large congregation, such as that of Theodore of Mopsuestia in late fourth-century Antioch, 'Everyone gives peace as far as possible to his neighbour . . . If the one who has been sinned against be near, he should put in practice the order of Christ literally'; whereas if the person were absent, or on the other side of the building, the offender must act upon an inner intention to make peace as soon as possible.[9]

A century and a half earlier in Syria, the community of the *Didascalia Apostolorum*—whose building and congregation were much smaller than Theodore's—nevertheless had a clearly articulated liturgical and pastoral process to enable reconciliation both within and without worship. The *Didascalia*, to be sure, does not specifically relate these to the kiss of peace; but its conjoining of the deacon's admonition to reconciliation with the Matthew 5.23-24 text places it in the tradition of the other texts whose reference to 'the peace' is specific, and would seem to indicate that this community practised the kiss of peace. At the end of the 'prayers' and before the 'oblations', a deacon would declaim: 'Is there any one that keeps anything against his fellow?' Most members, at this point,

---

[1] See Eleanor Kreider, 'Let the Faithful Greet Each Other: The Kiss of Peace,' *Conrad Grebel Review* 5 (1987) pp.29-49.

[2] Justin, 1 *Apol* 65.

[3] Clement of Alexandria, *Paedagogus* 3.12. See also Athenagoras, *Legatio* 32.

[4] Phillips, *Ritual Kiss* pp.109, 143-144.

[5] *Didache* 14.2.

[6] Tertullian, *De Oratione* 11.

[7] Cyprian, *De Oratione dominica* 23; Eusebius, *Life of Constantine* 4.41; Cyril of Jerusalem, *Mystagogic Homily* 5.3; John Chrysostom, *De Compunctione ad Demetrium* 1.3; Theodore of Mopsuestia, *Baptismal Homily* 4.40.

[8] Theodore of Mopsuestia, *Baptismal Homily* 4.6. See also Cyril of Jerusalem, *Mystagogic Homily* 5.3.

[9] Theodore of Mopsuestia, *Baptismal Homily* 4.39, 41.

would probably exchange an embrace celebrating the peace which God had given them through the Spirit. But if there were any that were quarrelling with each other, the bishop, as the church's peacemaker, was to call both parties—'for we do not call them brothers until peace has been made between them'—into his presence. A process of mediation ensued, with the aim of restoring right relationships by the following Lord's Day.[1]

Why all this procedure? After all, it, along with the transfer of gifts which was going on simultaneously, 'probably took a bit of time and caused considerable confusion.'[2] It was because of a widely-held early Christian conviction that a community of peace could only worship with integrity when it is at peace: 'if then you keep any malice against your brother, or he against you, your prayer is not heard and your eucharist is not accepted.' This procedure was also important because the Christian community only had something novel to offer the world when it was at peace: 'If then you preach peace to others, still more should you have peace with your brethren. As a son of light and peace therefore, be light and peace to all men . . . Be . . . peaceable one with another, and strive like wise doves to fill the church, and to convert and tame those that are wild and bring them into her midst.'[3] Because 'evangelism as well as Christian worship depended upon right relationships, it was vital that believers should observe the 'kiss of peace'.

---

[1] *Didascalia Apostolorum* 2.54.
[2] Robert Taft, *The Great Entrance: A History of the Transfer of Gifts and other Pre-anaphoral Rites of the Liturgy of St. John Chrysostom*, Orientalia Christiana Analecta, 200 (Pont. Institutum Studiorum Orientalium, Rome, 1975) p.50.
[3] *Didascalia Apostolorum* 2.53-54. For other pre-Christendom texts about the peace, see Justin, 1 *Apol* 65; Tertullian, *De oratione* 18; *idem*, *Ad Uxorem* 2.4; *Apostolic Tradition* 18; Cyprian, *De oratione dominica* 23; Origen, *Homilies on Romans* 10.33.

17. The Prayers: Interceding in Unity

The same qualities of peace and unity were fostered by the congregational prayers. The subject matter dealt with by the prayers of the people was rarely specified. The great exception—the prayer in 1 Clement—includes, amidst thanksgivings, two areas of petition that were probably common. There was prayer for the everyday needs of the Christian community: 'Rescue those of our number in distress; raise up the fallen; assist the needy; heal the sick; turn back those of your people who stray; feed the hungry; release our captives; revive the weak; encourage those who lose heart.' There also was prayer for the peace and and welfare of the empire and for 'our rulers and governors on earth.'[2] In Justin's Rome prayer for the emperor was a means by which a community accused of madness interceded for the sanity of its imperial persecutors.[2] Indeed, prayers for emperors, enemies, persecutors and for the Jews seem to have been common themes in early Christian assemblies.[3] In all of this there was a concern for what A. Hamman has called 'existential prayer'.[4] It was prayer which spanned the range of human experience and enabled the believers to do the difficult task of being both good citizens and 'keepers of what is commanded.'[5]

As they prayed the people customarily stood, with hands upraised. Tertullian, some of us may be glad to note, urged his friends to 'pray with modesty and humility, with not even our hands too loftily elevated, but elevated temperately and becomingly.'[6] But posture in prayer was not the main point; it was the peace and unity of the people praying. 'The place where the faithful congregate,' Origen contended, 'is especially conducive to prayer and makes it more effectual.' But, as Tertullian observed, prayer could be ineffectual, even 'lost', if it was marred by anger and broken relationships.[7] The *Didascalia Apostolorum* reminded its readers: ' . . . those who bear anger and malice towards their brethren God does not hear; and though you pray three times in one hour, you shall gain nothing, for you are not heard by reason of your enmity against your brother.'[8] Bad relationships meant ineffectual prayer.

---

[1] 1 Clement, *Ep* 59.2-61.3.
[2] Justin, *1 Apol* 17.
[3] Justin, *Dial* 96, 133; *1 Apol* 14; Tertullian, *Apol* 39.2; *Didascalia Apostolorum* 5.14; 5.16.
[4] A. Hamman, La Prière, II: *Les trois premiers siècles* (Desclée, Tournai, 1963) p.109.
[5] Justin, *1 Apol* 65.
[6] Tertullian, *De Oratione* 17; cf. Origen, *On Prayer* 31.2.
[7] Tertullian, *De Oratione* 11.
[8] *Didascalia Apostolorum* 2.53.

18. The Eucharist:
A Multi-Voiced Celebration

The eucharist, too, which the pre-Christendom communities celebrated every Sunday, could be marred or lost if there was an absence of unity. This was a time when the community's thanksgivings could well up. A typical eucharistic prayer might remember the suffering of the Lord Jesus Christ 'on behalf of those who are purified in soul from all iniquity;' it would also praise God for 'having created the world . . . for the sake of man, and for delivering us from the evil in which we were, and for utterly overthrowing principalities and powers by him who suffered according to [God's] will.'[1] Generally in the pre-Christendom period these prayers were expressed impromptu— 'not saying it word for word'—but within the tradition; often they were offered on behalf of the community by the presiding elder.[2]

But, as Marcel Metzger has pointed out, the manuscripts in various languages lying behind the 'reconstructed' chapter 9 of the *Apostolic Tradition* make it seem possible that the eucharistic prayer, far from being an episcopal solo as a 'reconstructed' text such as that of Dom Botte would seem to indicate, was a time when many could pray.[3] The variant texts of the *Apostolic Tradition* urge bishops not to discourage unrehearsed participation.[4] Someone in the congregation, according to the Sahidic (Coptic) text, might pray a 'glorious prayer', or, according to the Arabic text, pray a 'noble, outstanding prayer'. Others will pray shorter prayers, recite 'a hymn' (Arabic), or 'pray and say "glory" [or better: praise]' (Ethiopic). All of the versions, no doubt in sensitivity to the concerns of the bishops, stipulate that these spontaneous contributions be 'in measure' (i.e., not too long?), 'suited to his powers', or 'with moderation'. They also urge that the prayers be 'sound and orthodox.'

---

[1] Justin, *Dial* 41. See also the eucharistic prayer, so influential in modern times, in *Apostolic Tradition* 4.

[2] *Apostolic Tradition* 5, 9. Justin reported that the president would 'offer prayers and thanksgivings to the best of his ability' (1 *Apol* 67). Benedictine scholar Allen Bouley has established that it was only in the mid-fourth century that fixed formulae became usual (*From Freedom to Formula: The Evolution of the Eucharistic Prayer from Oral Improvisation to Written Texts*, The Catholic University of America Studies in Christian Antiquity, 21 (Catholic University of America Press, Washington, D.C., 1981) p.208. The *Didascalia Apostolorum* (2.58) even seems to indicate that, when a bishop from another congregation came as a visitor, the eucharistic prayer might be divided, with the visitor being allowed to 'speak over the cup'. For comment about what this might have entailed, see Paul Bradshaw, *Liturgical Presidency in the Early Church* (Grove Books, Bramcote, Notts, 1983) p.26.

[3] Widely used 'reconstructions' include Gregory Dix, *The Apostolic Tradition of St Hippolytus*, 2nd ed, rev H. Chadwick (SPCK, London, 1968); Bernard Botte, *La Tradition apostolique de Saint Hippolyte: Essaie de reconstitution*, Liturgiewissenschaftliche Quellen und Forschungen, 39, 3rd ed (Aschendorff, Münster, 1989); G. J. Cuming, *Hippolytus: A Text for Students*, Grove Liturgical Studies 8 (Grove Books, Bramcote, Notts, 1976). For illuminating discussion of the tendency of 'reconstitutions' to oversimplify (with special attention to the reconstitution of Dom Botte), see Marcel Metzger, 'Nouvelles perspectives pour la prétendue *Tradition Apostolique*' in *Ecclesia Orans* 5 (1988) pp.241-259; *idem*, 'Enquêtes' pp.7-36, esp p.9.

[4] For what follows, see Jean Michel Hanssens, *La Liturgie d'Hippolyte: Documents et Etudes* (Libreria Editrice dell'Università Gregoriana, Rome, 1970) pp.88-89, who provides Latin translations of the various texts. For chapter 9 of the *Apostolic Tradition* (Dix chapter 10), there are surviving manuscripts in Sahidic, Arabic and Ethiopic; the Latin is missing. I am grateful to Mr. G. Nussbaum of Keele University for his help with these texts.

These texts indicate that, in some communities, the eucharistic prayer(s) must have been a source of tension. One can imagine that some bishops in growing congregations were keen to keep things economical in word and time, while some members, aware that they had to get to their jobs, figuratively looked at their watches; meanwhile other members were eager to express their praises as part of a congregationally-uttered multi-voiced prayer. The eucharist was, after all, a unitive rite, the focus of the community's common adoration. It was a time of energetic corporate participation—' . . . all the people present sing out their assent by saying "Amen" . . .'[1]—and very possibly the time of its greatest fervour and spiritual concentration.[2]

But this concentration once again could be subverted if relationships were not right. The most important of God's precepts, according to Tertullian, was 'that we not go up unto God's altar before we have contracted [made peace] with our brethren. For what sort of deed is it to approach the peace of God without peace?'[3] Cyprian expressed this concern with equal intensity. God commands us, he says, 'to be peacemakers, and in agreement, and in one mind in his house.' He united us through baptism, and he wants us 'when new-born to continue' in unity so that the community may be a community of peace. God cares about this so passionately, Cyprian argued, that he 'does not receive the sacrifice of a person who is in disagreement, but commands him to go back from the altar and first be reconciled to his brother . . . Our peace and brotherly agreement is the greater sacrifice to God . . .'[4] A rite by itself, Cyprian was convinced, was wrong. As he added in another treatise, ' . . . it is of small account to be baptized and to receive the eucharist, unless one profit by it both in deeds and works.'[5] The pastoral purpose of worship was to empower a distinctive people.

---

[1] Justin, 1 *Apol* 65, transl Everett Ferguson, *Early Christians Speak* (Sweet Publishing Co., Austin, TX, 1971) p.94.
[2] Bardy, *Conversion* p.285.
[3] Tertullian, *De Oratione* 11.
[4] Cyprian, *De Oratione dominica* 24.
[5] Cyprian, *Ad Quirinum* 3.26.

19. The Offertory:
Shaping a Sharing People

The same aim of developing a community of freedom and peace animated the slowly developing rite of the offering. From the earliest times Christian writers expressed their concern about the power of wealth to destroy souls and relationships; they also, throughout the early centuries, expressed their desire to live as free people. Irenaeus rejoiced in the work of 'our Liberator' Christ, who had freed him and his fellow Christians to go beyond the demands of Old Testament law: 'instead of the law enjoining the giving of tithes, [he told us] to share all our possessions with the poor.'[1] A similar reservation about the tithe is found in other early Christian writing. The tithe was not free: the early Christians put a strong emphasis upon *voluntary* giving. It also was too little: Jesus had told his followers, 'Sell all that you have, and give to the poor.'[2] Why then give? Because, according to Cyprian, people's possessions possess them and deprive them of freedom.[3] In his *De Lapsis* he even noted a clear correlation between wealth and apostasy.[4] The early Christians, from Barnabas and the Didache through to Tertullian, found it to be good news that the Christians 'share everything with [their] brother and call nothing [their] own.'[5] This did not mean that in their communities private property was abolished; it did mean that because the fear that leads to accumulation was being addressed, people were free to share, free to give radically to church funds which were used to support poorer members, widows and orphans, prisoners, other congregations, even non-Christians.[6] This, the Christians were aware, was good news. Outsiders, from philosophers like Galen to their immediate neighbours, watched them in amazement. ' "Look," they say, "how they love one another." '[7]

During our period a rite gradually developed—the offering—which nurtured this generosity in worship. At first Christians evidently gave their gifts directly to the needy sister or brother, or to the to the congregational common funds via the bishops or deacons as intermediaries. But by the second century such giving was done in the context of of their Sunday services. Tertullian reported that in his community in Carthage this happened once a month; in Rome, according to Justin, it seems to have happened weekly.[8] People would come to worship bringing money, and also in some communities food (in the *Apostolic Tradition* 5-6 there are prayers of blessing for oil, cheese and olives as well as bread and wine). From this food the deacons would take the bread and wine which the president would use in the eucharist. By the late third century it is clear that

---

[1] Irenaeus, *Adversus Haereses* 5.13.3; see also 4.17.5; 4.18.2; 4.34.4.

[2] Cyprian, *De opere et eleemosynis* 7; *Didascalia Apostolorum* 2.35; (Victor?), *De Aleatoribus* 11 ('Divert all your fortune and surplus for the necessities of the Church.'), in Scott T. Carroll, 'An Early Church Sermon Against Gambling,' *Second Century* 8 (1991) p.94.

[3] Cyprian, *De opere et eleemosynis* 13.

[4] Cyprian, *De Lapsis* 6.

[5] Barnabas, *Ep* 19.8; *Didache* 4.8; Tertullian, *Apol* 39.11.

[6] Eusebius, *HE* 4.23.10; 6.34.11.

[7] Tertullian, *Apol* 39.7; on Galen, see Robert Wilken, *The Christians as the Romans Saw Them* (Yale University Press, New Haven, 1984) pp.79-82.

[8] Tertullian, *Apol* 39.5; Justin, 1 *Apol* 67.

people were bringing gifts of clothing and shoes as well.[1] Everyone, even the poorest, was admonished to 'come to the Lord's Supper [with] a sacrifice.'[2] Precise details are lacking for this period, but it seems that as the people entered the church building they deposited their varied offerings on a table by the entrance.[3] The deacons, who superintended the process, then took some food forward for use in the eucharist; the other gifts they deposited with the community's leader, who, as 'the protector of all in need,' was responsible for the community's varied ministries.[4] Not to give in such a setting was to deny communion, and thereby to undermine the community's common ethos. The offering was a worship rite for a distinctive community, a people being liberated from the addiction of accumulation and freed for 'sharing' and 'magnanimity.'[5]

---

[1] *Gesta apud Zenophilum* 3, in MacMullen and Lane (eds) *Paganism and Christianity*, p.249. For futher examples of the varied nature of gifts, see Joseph A. Jungmann, *The Mass of the Roman Rite: Its Origins and Development*, transl Francis A. Brunner (Four Courts Press, Dublin, 1986) II p.10; Taft, *The Great Entrance* p.17n.

[2] Cyprian, *De opere et eleemosynis* 15; *Didascalia Apostolorum* 2.36; 5.1. For comment, see A. Hamman, *Vie liturgique et vie sociale* (Desclée, Paris, 1968) p.265.

[3] *Didascalia Apostolorum* 2.57. For the early development of the offertory in East and in Rome, see Taft, *Great Entrance* pp.11-34; Jungmann, *Mass of the Roman Rite* II pp.1-10.

[4] Justin, 1 *Apol* 67.

[5] Cyprian, *De opere et eleemosynis* 15, 20, 26.

20. The Sermons: Exhorting Christians lest Pagans 'mock at the Name'

We conclude our examination of the components of early Christian worship by going back to the part of the service that the catechumens could experience along with the believers—the sermon.[1] It is dangerous to use the word 'sermon' during the pre-Christendom period, for both 'sermon' and 'preaching' have come for us to connote one speaker addressing a passive congregation, sometimes at considerable length.[2] This was a phenomenon which few pre-Christendom Christians would have recognized. Let us recall the setting of early Christian Sunday worship: a smallish gathering of people, who know each other well, and who meet in a quasi-domestic space[3] early in the morning for an hour or so before going to work.[4] (The Sunday holiday is a Christendom institution, dating from 321.) In this service, in addition to the readings and address, there would be prayers and the eucharist. The time for the address would thus be limited, typically to less than a half an hour.[5] And the person giving the address would speak on intimate terms with people for whose common life in a situation of pressure he was responsible. In this setting, the early Latin sermon 'Concerning the Dice-Players' (by Bishop Victor of Rome?) is right at home. It is modest in length (21 minutes), laced with appeals to scripture and both practical and hortatory: 'I ask you, O Christian . . .'[6] Melito of Sardis's so-called sermon *On the Pascha*, on the other hand, fits less well. At 36 minutes it is somewhat on the long side; and its 'extravagant rhetorical forms' are much too polished and literarily dense to have communicated to a typical congregation in Sardis.[7] Origen's *Homilies on Luke*, by way of contrast, are much shorter, and more straightforward and accessible, than Melito's 'sermon'. On average only a third of the length of his Old Testament homilies (which he delivered in daily catechetical sessions), Origen's Lucan

---

[1] For general treatments of the sermon in early Christianity, see Thomas K. Carroll, *Preaching the Word*, Message of the Fathers of the Church, 11 (Michael Glazier, Wilmington, Delaware, 1984); Carl A. Volz, *Pastoral Life and Practice in the Early Church* (Augsburg, Minneapolis, 1990) chap. 3.

[2] I have benefited from reading the illuminating, and as yet unpublished, MS of D. C. Norrington, *The Sermon in the Early Church and Today*.

[3] In the period after the Decian persecution, some Christian communities became large, with substantial purpose-built buildings to house their eucharistic services. See Eusebius, *HE* 8.1; White, *Building God's House* pp.127-139.

[4] 'We get up at daybreak and pray God to be able to eat the crumbs which fall from his table' (Origen, *Homilies on Luke* 38.6).

[5] Alexandre Olivar, *La Predicación Cristiana Antigua*, Biblioteca Herder, Sección de Teología y Filosofía, 189 (Editorial Herder, Barcelona, 1991) p.51 (I have not had the time, or the linguistic competence, to do justice to this imposing work). In the 370s Basil of Caesarea was still aware of time constraints for his weekday-morning homilies: 'It has not escaped my notice that many artisans, employed in manual labours and who earn just enough at their daily work to provide for their own nourishment, are surrounding me and obliging me to be brief, so I shall not keep them too long from their jobs' (*Homilies on the Hexameron* 3.1).

[6] Carroll, 'An Early Church Sermon Against Gambling' pp.83-95, esp 88 and 90.

[7] S. G. Hall (ed) *Melito of Sardis on Pascha and Fragments* (Clarendon Press, Oxford, 1979) p.xix.

homilies were designed for delivery in a Sunday eucharistic service.[1] We must remember, however, that nothing that Origen did can be construed as typical!

For helpful insight on the role of instruction in a typical congregation we can turn to Justin's first *Apology*. From this we learn that in a service in mid-second-century Rome, after readings from the 'memoirs of the apostles' and the 'writings of the prophets . . . as long as time permits,' the community's leader would then 'in a discourse [*dia logou*] urge and invite [his hearers] to the imitation of these noble things.'[2] Here we have a pattern— a single speaker who is the communal 'president', expounding a biblical passage, and applying it to the life of his community. Liturgical scholars caution us not to generalize too confidently on Justin,[3] but in this case I think his pattern was probably widespread. It's not that there was generally only one speaker. The background of the Jewish synagogue, as well as that of 1 Corinthians 14, would point to the participation of a number of speakers.[4] Tertullian, reporting on worship in Carthage, speaks of 'exhortation in our gatherings, rebuke, divine censure': clearly in his church the exhortations addressed the life of the congregation, but he does not say how many people spoke.[5]

Perhaps the document that helps us most to come to terms with early preaching is the so-called 'Second Letter of Clement.' This anonymous second-century document, whose place of writing is debated, is clearly a sermon.[6] 'Clement' comments that in a typical service in his community the elders (he does not say how many) would exhort the people. But on this occasion he, 'after God's truth' (the biblical reading), is 'reading you an exhortation to heed what was there written.' *Reading* an exhortation, by *one* person: obviously this is a departure from the norm, which would be the impromptu exhortations of several elders.[7] But, although the form may have been unusual, 'Clement's' subject matter would seem to have been typical. His concern was to keep the Christian community that he was addressing on course. He dealt with problems facing the community—the deferring of the *parousia*, a cooling of faith among people whose parents had been Christian, a creeping love of money.[8] He expressed concern about the community's witness. Neighbours, he reported, who 'hear God's oracles on our lips . . .

---

[1] P. Nautin (*Origène* p.397) explained the brevity of Origen's Lucan homilies by positing the existence of *three* Sunday homilies in Caesarea which together would equal the length of one weekday homily. If on Sunday there were other homilies, the other two were likely to have been much shorter than Origen's. It was inconvenient for the Sunday eucharistic services to get too long—after all, people had to work; and the non-instructional components of the Sunday service in my view took longer than Nautin thought.

[2] Justin, 1 *Apol* 67.

[3] Bradshaw, *The Search for the Origins* pp.139-140.

[4] E. P. Sanders, *Judaism, Practice and Belief, 66 BCE-66 CE* (SCM Press, London, 1992) p.202.

[5] Tertullian, *Apol* 39.3-4.

[6] As to the place of origin of 2 Clement, C. C. Richardson proposes Egypt (*Early Christian Fathers*, Library of Christian Classics, I (Westminster Press, Philadelphia, 1953) p.186); P. F. Beatrice says Syria or possibly Egypt (*Encyclopedia of the Early Church*, I p.181); Robert M. Grant is confident of Rome (*The Apostolic Fathers* (Thomas Nelson, New York, 1965) II p.109), as is Graydon F. Snyder (in Everett Ferguson, ed. *Encyclopedia of Early Christianity* (Garland, New York, 1990) p.217).

[7] 2 Clement, *Ep* 17.3, 5; 19.1.

[8] *Ibid.* 11.2-3; 12.1; 20.1.

marvel at their beauty and greatness.' But when they note that we don't live what we say, they scoff at Christian teaching as 'a myth and a delusion.'

'When, for instance, they hear from us that God says, "It is no credit to you if you love those who love you, but it is to your credit if you love your enemies and those who hate you," when they hear these things, they are amazed at such surpassing goodness. But when they see that we fail to love not only those who hate us, but even those who love us, then they mock at us and scoff at the Name.'[1]

Jesus' teaching, 'Clement' was reminding the congregation, was a part of their evangelism. Pagans found this new, intriguing, beautiful. But when people saw that the Christian community wasn't living what it taught, this lack of integrity was an impediment to its witness. In light of this, 'Clement's' call to the Church was to return to fundamentals—to be true to their baptismal commitments: to 'do holy and upright deeds'; to have faith; and above all, 'Let us . . . love one another, so that we may all come to God's Kingdom.'[2]

We don't know whether Clement would have been interrupted in mid-flow, asking him what he meant by *this*, or how the church could do *that*. Certainly there is evidence that such interruptions could take place in the early sermons.[3] Furthermore, the words *dialegou* and *dialexis* have obvious etymological components indicating dialogue; and the Latin *sermo* denoted 'exchange of talk betwen two or more speakers, conversation, dialogue.'[4] If there was a dialogical component in 'Clement's' address, it would have enabled him to express his concern—the shaping of the character of a community so that it applied the message and teachings of Jesus to its practical circumstances—in a community-forming medium.

Further evidence of a sermon—applying the Bible to a community's life—comes from Cyprian's life as reported by his biographer Pontius. In 250-251 the Decian persecution had led to the deaths of some Carthaginian Christians and the apostasy of many more. Later in 251 came the great plague, possibly of measles, which ecumenically killed pagans and Christians alike. Wealthy pagans were 'shuddering, fleeing, shunning the contagion.'[5] Carcases were piling up in the city. What should the Christians do? Cyprian, according to Pontius, urged the Christian community to be true to their calling. Having described God's goodness and mercy, he then turned to the community members in their setting. He observed

'that there was nothing wonderful in our cherishing our own people only with the needed attentions of love, but that he might become perfect who would do

---

[1] *Ibid*. 13.3-4.

[2] *Ibid*. 6.9; 20.1.

[3] Norrington, *The Sermon in the Early Church*, 10, 34, 110; J. Heinemann, 'Preaching, in the Talmudic Period,' in *Encyclopaedia Judaica*, 13 (Keter Publishing House, Jerusalem, 1971) cols 995-996; Maurice Sachot, 'Homilie', *Reallexikon für Antike und Christentum*, 16 (1991-1992) cols 159-160; G. Wright Doyle, 'Augustine's Sermonic Method' in *Westminster Theological Journal* 39 (1976-1977) p.236; F. Van der Meer, *Augustine the Bishop: The Life and Work of a Father of the Church*, transl Brian Battershaw and G. R. Lamb (Sheed and Ward, London, 1961) pp.427-428; Hippolytus, *Comm on Daniel* 3.20-25; Origen, *Homilies on Jeremiah* 1.7; 1.8; 5.13; John Chrysostom, *Homilies against the Jews* 1.7; Egeria, *Travels* 46.4.

[4] G. W. H. Lampe (ed.) *A Patristic Greek Lexikon* (Clarendon Press, Oxford, 1965) p.355; P. G. W. Glare (ed.) *Oxford Latin Dictionary* (Clarendon Press, Oxford, 1982) p.1743; Albert Blaise, *Dictionnaire Latin-Français des Auteurs Chrétiens* (Le Latin Chrétien, Strasbourg, 1954) p.755.

[5] Pontius, *Vita Cypriani* 9.

something more than the publican or the heathen, who, overcoming evil with good, and practising a clemency which was like the divine clemency, loved even his enemies, who would pray for the salvation of those that persecute him, as the Lord admonishes and exhorts. God continually makes his sun to rise, and from time to time gives showers to nourish the seed, exhibiting all these kindnesses not only to his people but to aliens also. And if a man professes to be a son of God, why does he not imitate the example of his Father. "It becomes us," said he, "to answer to our birth . . ." '[1]

In a situation of danger and plague, Cyprian's sermon was a call to his community to act in light of its catechism. It had been loved into existence by God whose plan has ensured that its dead 'are alive with God.'[2] It had been given a distinctive way to live by Jesus. And here Cyprian, applying Matthew 5.43-48 to this desperately dangerous situation, was urging his friends not to save their own lives, not even to ensure that the Christian community would survive, but rather to act differently from the pagans. This was an opportunity for the Christians to love their enemies who recently had been persecuting them. They could do so by staying in Carthage and nursing pagan and Christian alike. Christians could do this because they, unlike the pagans, can anticipate 'the pleasure . . . [of] the heavenly kingdom, without fear of death.'[3] A recent study has postulated the missionary effectiveness of this policy. The minority Christian community, which did not flee but stayed to provide nursing, had a higher survival rate than their pagan neighbours; and the pagans who had been nursed through the crisis by Christians were likely to be open to a faith that, unlike their own, had worked.[4]

[1] *Ibid.*
[2] Cyprian, *De mortalitate* 20.
[3] *Ibid.* 26.
[4] Rodney Stark, 'Epidemics, Networks, and the Rise of Christianity,' pp.159-175. For comparable events in Alexandria in 260, see Eusebius, *HE* 7.22.2-10.

21. The Advent of Christendom

So Christianity grew in pre-Christendom. When functioning at its best, the church's worship was shaping a people whose life, and whose response to the world, were distinctive.

When then did Christendom begin?[1] Already in the third century, and with increasing momentum in the fourth century, major changes were occurring. Origen, speaking before the Decian persecution, sorrowfully questioned whether 'the crowds we see assembled . . . [were] real believers at all.'[2] Noting the respect in which 'rich men and persons in positions of honour and ladies of refinement and high birth' held the Christians, Origen speculated that 'some might become leaders of the Christian teaching for the sake of a little prestige.'[3] In the period 260-303, after the collapse of Valerian's persecution, the church grew still more rapidly; some scholars, developing a theme of W. H. C. Frend, have viewed this period as 'The Triumph of Christianity'. The 'Great Persecution' of 303-312, in this perspective, was terrifying and at times lethal, but was ultimately a desperate attempt by petrified pagans to roll back the seemingly irreversible expansion of Christianity.[4] Other scholars have placed more emphasis upon the role of the Emperor Constantine I in the advent of Christendom.[5] In 312 Constantine was converted, bringing the toleration for which the Christians had longed. In the course of his long reign he made Christianity the way to get ahead in respectable circles. As disincentives disappeared and incentives appeared, the church grew even more rapidly; estimates vary, but one scholar has hazarded that by the end of the fourth century up to one half of the imperial populace was Christian.[6] By 392, when Emperor Theodosius I outlawed any public worship but that of orthodox Christianity, the components of Christendom were firmly in place—a civilization professing Christian values, supported by an all-encompassing state-related church, and marked by coercion and an absence of choice.

---

[1] Judith Herrin (*The Formation of Christendom* (Princeton University Press, 1987)) does not define Christendom. But on p.479, in writing of its collapse, she gives two of its essential ingredients: 'the dominance of religion' coupled with an absence of 'choice'.

[2] Origen, *Hom on Jeremiah* 4.3.

[3] Origen, *Contra Celsum* 3.9. For an illuminating survey of third-century church life which may underestimate the extent of the Christians' distinctiveness, see Wischmeyer, *Von Golgatha zum Ponte Molle, passim.*

[4] W. H. C. Frend, *Martyrdom and Persecution in the Early Church* (Basil Blackwell, Oxford, 1965) p.440; T. D. Barnes, 'Christians and Pagans in the Reign of Constantius,' in Albrecht Dihle (ed) *L'Eglise et l'empire au iv* siècle, Entretiens sur l'antiquité classique, 34 (Fondation Hardt, Vandoeuvres-Geneva, 1989) p.307.

[5] MacMullen, *Christianizing* p 102; Lane Fox, *Pagans and Christians* p.609.

[6] MacMullen, *Christianizing* p.85.

22. Church Growth and the Atrophy of Catechism

It was predictable: the proscription of non-Christian worship and the coupling of Christianity with career prospects, accompanied by the destruction of pagan shrines, led to further church growth. Christianity, by the process which Sir Herbert Butterfield called 'inducement and compulsion,' was now the unrivalled religion of the Roman Empire.[1] And, inevitably, over the course of several centuries both the means and the meaning of becoming a Christian gradually changed. A papyrus from early fourth-century Egypt provides a clue: 'a form letter for recommending catechumens, with the name entered later'.[2] At least in the community which produced this document, routine had superceded scrutiny in the reception of candidates for baptism. The time allotted for catechism also shortened—from the three years of the *Apostolic Tradition* to, at most, the Lenten season. Furthermore, as time went on the catechists who have left literary records seem to have felt that it was less important to instruct baptismal candidates in the history and folkways of a new community than in orthodox doctrine and the sacramental mysteries. Although in Antioch John Chrysostom still dealt with issues of practical discipleship, in Nyssa Gregory's *Catechetical Oration* was preoccupied with the nuances of orthodoxy—he devoted only a few incidental sentences to the behavioural signs of being 'only seemingly, and not really, regenerate.'[3] In Jerusalem, Cyril's concerns were almost entirely doctrinal and mystagogical.[4]

This shift of emphasis becomes clear when one compares Basil of Caesarea, writing in Asia Minor the 370s, with Augustine, writing in North Africa a generation later. Basil insisted that 'one must first be made a disciple before being admitted to baptism', which meant—in such practical areas as wealth and violence—instructing the catechumens about ways of living differently from 'the pagans and the people who are in the world.' Augustine, on the other hand, declared that 'first one should baptize them; thereafter one should instruct them over a change in lifestyle and customs.'[5] As this situation evolved, the baptism of infants spread; in 529 Justinian I made it imperial law, and by the eighth century it had everywhere become the norm.[6] The parents and godparents of the

---

[1] Sir Herbert Butterfield, *Christianity and History* (Charles Scribner's Sons, New York, 1949) p.135. MacMullen more colourfully has called the process 'flattery and battery' (*Christianizing* p.119).

[2] E. A. Judge, 'The Earliest Use of Monachos for "Monk" ' in *Jahrbuch für Antike und Christentum* 20 (1977) p.81.

[3] John Chrysostom, *Baptismal Instructions* 9.36-47; Gregory of Nyssa, *Catechetical Oration* 40.

[4] Cyril of Jerusalem, *Procatechesis*; *Catechetical Lectures* 1-23.

[5] Basil of Caesarea, *On Baptism* 1.2.1, 11-12; Augustine, *Faith and Works* 9.

[6] *Codex Justinianus* 1.11.10. For the persistence of believers' baptism into the Christendom period, see A. Piédagnel (ed) *Jean Chrysostome: Trois catéchèses baptismales*, Sources Chrétiennes, 366 (Cerf, Paris, 1990) pp.256-257, who concludes that infant baptism in the Eastern and Western churches was available and was justified by some theologians but 'not generalized' in practice until the sixth century. A leading authority on early baptismal practice, the Rev. S. Anita Stauffer, points to 'abundant adult baptisms in the West until about the eighth century, although infant baptism was also practiced on an increasing basis (depending on what specific area is under consideration)' (personal communication, 10 March 1994). For the eventual effects upon the baptismal liturgy of the rise of infant baptism, see J-Ch Didier, 'Une Adaptation de la liturgie baptismale au baptême des enfants dans l'église ancienne' in *Mélanges de science religieuse* 22 (1965) pp.79-90.

infants may or may not have been able thereafter to catechize them. In situations in which large numbers of people were converting, the only means of catechizing them about behaviour was the sermon, now given to large congregations; and there is evidence that at least in some places those attending these constituted but a small proportion of the populace.[1] Despite the complaints of the preachers about their hearers' misbehaviour and commitment to 'the pleasures of the world', by the fifth century church leaders in most places seem to have assumed that the narratives and folkways of converts would continue largely unchanged.[2] From a pre-Christendom perspective, their conversion had been, at best, partial.

---

[1] Ramsay MacMullen, 'The Preacher's Audience (AD 350-400)' in *Journal of Theological Studies* n.s. 40 (1989) p.510.
[2] Cesarius of Arles, *Sermon* 73.2.

23. The Amplification of Worship

In the self-confessedly Christian world of Christendom, the Church became a dominant institution. Its worship changed, becoming characterized by what Orthodox liturgical theologian Alexander Schmemann has called 'amplification.'[1] We cannot trace these changes here; this would require another essay. Suffice it to say that in Christendom, as the numbers of worshippers grew, the relational aspects of pre-Christendom worship atrophied while the more ceremonial aspects flourished.[2] Symbolic of this was the withering of the peace and the efflorescence of another rite which took place at the same time—the offertory procession.[3] In ritual as well as setting the magnificent cult 'inculturated,' borrowed heavily from the imperial court, thereby functioning in 'the deployment and legitimation of social power.'[4] Of course, the elaborate worship, together with the clerical staff required to choreograph it, needed money to pay for it. This came from the tithe, which functioned as a kind of Christendom tax. In the West, the Second Council of Mâcon in 585, justifying its innovation by an appeal to 'ancient usage' which would have astonished Irenaeus, required Christians in Gaul, on pain of excommunication, to bring their tithes to those responsible for the worship of the church.[5]

---

[1] Alexander Schmemann, *Introduction to Liturgical Theology*, 2nd ed, trans. A. E. Moorhouse (Faith Press, Leighton Buzzard, 1975) p.93.

[2] Sample comparisons between the earlier church orders and the revisions in the late fourth-century *Apostolic Constitutions* indicate the flavour of the changes, from peacemaking relationships to a peaceable attitude: compare *Didache* 4.14 with *Apostolic Constitutions* 7.17; or *Didache* 14.2 with *Apostolic Constitutions* 7.30; or *Didascalia Apostolorum* 2.53 with *Apostolic Constitutions* 2.54: 'before all things, it is our duty to be at peace in our own minds . . .'

[3] Taft, *Great Entrance* pp.46-52.

[4] Johannes Quasten, 'Mysterium Tremendum: eucharistische Frömmigkeitsauffassungen des vierten Jahrhunderts,' in A. Mayr, J. Quasten and B. Neunheuser (eds) *Vom Christlichen Mysterium: Gesammelte Arbeiten zum Gedächtnis von Odo Casel* (Patmos Verlag, Düsseldorf, 1951) pp.71-74; Walter Brueggemann, *Israel's Praise: Doxology against Idolatry and Ideology* (Fortress Press, Philadelphia, 1989) p.ix.

[5] Second Council of Mâcon (585), canon 5, in J. Gaudemet and B. Basdevant (eds), *Les Canons des conciles Mérovingiens (VIe-VIe siècles)*, II, Sources Chrétiennes, 354 (Editions du Cerf, Paris, 1989) pp.462-463. The council fathers bewailed that 'at the present, little by little, almost all the Christians are showing themselves to be violators of the laws, neglecting to accomplish what has been fixed by God'. So they ordered that the 'primitive state' of the Church should be restored by requiring all the people to pay tithes to those in charge of the Church's worship.

24. Christendom Understandings of Peace and Identity

As the Christendom centuries progressed, some Christians confined the radical teachings of Jesus—such as those on wealth, to which Irenaeus had appealed—to a clerical or sectarian elite. Others handled them so as not to require Christians to behave unconventionally in their public lives.[1] In Christendom similar changes took place in the use of the 'swords into ploughshares' texts of Isaiah 2 and Micah 4.[2] In pre-Christendom, writers such as Irenaeus and Origen had appealed to these passages as evidence for the eschatological peace which Christian communities already experienced and which needed to be nurtured in worship and tended by appropriate folkways.[3] In early fifth-century Christendom, on the other hand, Cyril of Alexandria applied the texts not to the church but to the Empire; within it swords had been beaten into ploughshares because 'many peoples were . . . conquered by Roman weapons and so converted.'[4] Anticipatory of the Christendom approach in the West was Augustine of Hippo. Not once did he cite these passages which had been so important to the pre-Christendom writers.[5] But in his commentary on the Psalms he addressed other passages, such as Psalm 46.10: 'He makes war cease to the ends of the earth.' 'This text,' Augustine wrote, 'has not yet been fulfilled . . . There are wars between factions, wars between the Jews, the pagans, the Christians, the heretics.' Only in the hearts of reconciled individuals, or in heaven, will we discover the peace that we long for on earth.[6]

In this Christendom world, the understandings of the early Christians were transformed and their vocabulary took on new meanings. In Christendom, for example, Christians were still called *paroikoi/parochiani*, but the term no longer meant resident aliens. It now meant residents, parishioners, people whose distinctiveness was not that they were unlike their neighbours, but that they were unlike people in other countries whose rulers espoused some other faith. Where everyone was a Christian, their primary allegiances was no longer to the transnational family of God; it rather was to people with whom they shared a common race and place. So the internationalism of early Christianity was superseded by localism; already in the 370s Basil of Caesarea was detecting a 'solitariness' in which the Cappadocian Christians 'sever ourselves from the whole world'.[7]

---

[1] Loyd Allen, 'The Sermon on the Mount in the History of the Church,' *Review and Expositor* 89 (1992) pp.245-262.

[2] For what follows, see Lohfink, ' "Schwerter zu Pflugscharen" ' pp.197-202.

[3] Irenaeus, *Adversus Haereses* 4.34.4; Origen, *Contra Celsum* 5.33. I will not discuss here the vexed question of the pre-Christendom Christians and warfare. For a review of recent literature, see David G. Hunter, 'A Decade of Research on Early Christians and Military Service' in *Religious Studies Review* 18,2 (April 1992) 87-94.

[4] Cyril of Alexandria, *Commentary on Isaiah*, 2.4.

[5] Lohfink, ' "Schwerter zu Pflugscharen" ' 202.

[6] Augustine, *Enarr in ps.* 46.10; 48.17.

[7] Basil of Caesarea, *Epp.* 191, 203.2.

25. Worship and Evangelism in Post-Christendom

Whatever the benefits of Christendom—and there were many—we today are no longer living in Christendom. The grand edifice built on coercive Christianity has crumbled, and in many Western countries it is now a counter-cultural act to go to church. Some people in fact now view themselves explicitly as pagan. These people view Christianity as a kind of parenthesis in Western history, which will inevitably be replaced by a religion that is more authentically European—paganism. Those of us who believe otherwise are aware that Christianity is on trial in the West. If the church survives, it will not be because of its power to coerce. Nor will it be because its worship continues— as if nothing had changed—to struggle along in its Christendom ruts. Christianity will rather survive because God's Spirit is enabling Christians to worship so they will live, not as mere residents but, as in the early centuries, as resident aliens, imaginative disciples of Jesus who are purveyors of good news to our time.

I believe that worship can nurture people today, as it nurtured the pre-Christendom Christians, to be missionaries in our culture. And I sense that, if we are attentive and imaginative, the worship of the early Church may help our churches as we search for a renewal of rite and practice. In German the early Church is called *die Alte Kirche*—the old Church. Is it possible that, as we engage in dialogue with it, the old Church can help us, even in post-Christendom, to follow Jesus in a Church that is perennially young?

Alcuin/GROW Joint Liturgical Studies

All cost £3.95 (US $8) in 1995

1987 TITLES

1. **(LS 49) Daily and Weekly Worship—from Jewish to Christian**
   by Roger Beckwith, Warden of Latimer House, Oxford
2. **(LS 50) The Canons of Hippolytus**
   edited by Paul Bradshaw, Professor of Liturgics, University of Notre Dame
3. **(LS 51) Modern Anglican Ordination Rites** edited by Colin Buchanan, then Bishop of Aston
4. **(LS 52) Models of Liturgical Theology** by James Empereur, of the Jesuit School of Theology, Berkeley

1988 TITLES

5. **(LS 53) A Kingdom of Priests: Liturgical Formation of the Laity: The Brixen Essays**
   edited by Thomas Talley, Professor of Liturgics, General Theological Seminary, New York.
6. **(LS 54) The Bishop in Liturgy: an Anglican Study** edited by Colin Buchanan, then Bishop of Aston
7. **(LS 55) Inculturation: the Eucharist in Africa**
   by Phillip Tovey, research student, previously tutor in liturgy in Uganda
8. **(LS 56) Essays in Early Eastern Initiation**
   edited by Paul Bradshaw, Professor of Liturgics, University of Notre Dame

1989 TITLES

9. **(LS 57) The Liturgy of the Church in Jerusalem** by John Baldovin
10. **(LS 58) Adult Initiation** edited by Donald Withey
11. **(LS 59) 'The Missing Oblation': The Contents of the Early Antiochene Anaphora** by John Fenwick
12. **(LS 60) Calvin and Bullinger on the Lord's Supper** by Paul Rorem

1990 TITLES

13-14 **(LS 61) The Liturgical Portions of The Apostolic Constitutions: A Text for Students**
   edited by W. Jardine Grisbrooke (This double-size volume, costs double price (i.e. £7.90 in 1995)).
15. **(LS 62) Liturgical Inculturation in the Anglican Communion**
   edited by David Holeton, Professor of Liturgics, Trinity College, Toronto
16. **(LS 63) Cremation Today and Tomorrow** by Douglas Davies, University of Nottingham

1991 TITLES

17. **(LS64) The Preaching Service—The Glory of the Methodists**
   by Adrian Burdon, Methodist Minister in Rochdale
18. **(LS65) Irenaeus of Lyon on Baptism and Eucharist**
   edited with Introduction, Translation and Commentary by David Power, Washington, D.C.
19. **(LS66) Testamentum Domini** edited by Grant Sperry-White, Department of Theology, Notre Dame
20. **(LS67) The Origins of the Roman Rite**
   Edited by Gordon Jeanes, then Lecturer in Liturgy, University of Durham

1992 TITLES

21. **The Anglican Eucharist in New Zealand 1814-1989**
   by Bosco Peters, Christchurch, New Zealand
22-23. **Foundations of Christian Music: The Music of Pre-Constantinian Christianity**
   by Edward Foley, Capuchin Franciscan, Chicago (second double-sized volume at £7.90 in 1995))

1993 TITLES

24. **Liturgical Presidency** by Paul James
25. **The Sacramentary of Sarapion of Thmuis: A Text for Students**
   edited by Ric Lennard-Barrett, West Australia
26. **Communion Outside the Eucharist** by Phillip Tovey, Banbury, Oxon.

1994 TITLES

27. **Revising the Eucharist: Groundwork for the Anglican Communion**
   edited by David Holeton, Dean of Trinity College, Toronto
28. **Anglican Liturgical Inculturation in Africa** edited by David Gitari, Bishop of Klrinyaga, Kenya
29-30. **On Baptismal Fonts: Ancient and Modern** by Anita Stauffer, Lutheran World Federation, Geneva
   (Double-sized volume at £7.90)

1995 TITLES

31. **The Comparative Liturgy of Anton Baumstark** by Fritz West
32. **Worship and Evangelism in Pre-Christendom** by Alan Kreider
33. **Worship in Ancient Egypt** by Maxwell Johnson (December 1995)